THE
DIGITAL
SALES
REP

Find and Close Your
Target Clients Online With
The 10 + 10 System

BE BOLD. BE VISIBLE.
BE UNSTOPPABLE.

To: Pruja

Thank you for the friendship
& business over the years.
Enjoy the Read!

Trudi

THE
DIGITAL
SALES
REP

Find and Close Your Target Clients Online With The 10 + 10 System

BE BOLD. BE VISIBLE. BE UNSTOPPABLE.

TRUDI CHAREST

Published by Best Seller Publishing®, St. Augustine, FL
Best Seller Publishing® is a registered trademark.
Printed in the United States of America.
ISBN: 978-1-956649-22-2

This p ublication i s d esigned t o p rovide a ccurate a nd a uthoritative i nformation w ith r egard t o the subject matter covered. It is sold with the understanding that the publisher is not engaged in rendering legal, accounting, or other professional advice. If legal advice or other expert assistance is required, the services of a competent professional should be sought. The opinions expressed by the authors in this book are not endorsed by Best Seller Publishing® and are the sole responsibility of the author rendering the opinion.

For more information, please write:
Best Seller Publishing®
53 Marine Street
St. Augustine, FL 32084
or call 1 (626) 765 9750
Visit us online at: www.BestSellerPublishing.org

Table of Contents

Foreword

Throughout my career and in the line of work I do, I have met hundreds of salespeople, marketers, and networkers. Some were mediocre, others were average, and only a select few were truly great. While each salesperson holds a unique skill set, there are clear characteristics and ingredients that are possessed by the top echelon of high performers. When I first met Trudi Charest, I saw something in her *completely different* from anyone I had ever met. She was tenacious, dedicated, intelligent, and resilient. It was during our very first lunch meeting that I found myself asking her to quit her lucrative vice president role and join me in creating and launching a marketing agency. I just knew that she was built differently.

In the first five years of building our business together, Trudi has demonstrated that she exists at a level all her own. She has taken on the primary role of business development within our company, and she continues to set new levels of expectations and results. I've watched her build her unique selling system, tweak it over the years, and ultimately perfect it. She consistently generates new leads each week (seemingly out of thin air) and closes new clients at a pace that is beyond comprehension.

What I know to be true is that a great system will elevate an average salesperson, while a mediocre system will limit someone great to being simply average. The selling system that Trudi Charest has created provides the framework, direction, and tangible action items for anybody to become that great salesperson who can constantly, sustainably, and predictably grow their prospect databases and close leads. If you follow it, you'll have the tools required to find success in your selling career, as Trudi has in hers.

Each chapter begins with a personal anecdote or story that helps the reader contextualize the importance of the chapter ahead. Trudi then goes on to provide tangible instructions on building the ideal selling system, before finishing with an itemized list of actionable steps to take. Building and following her system is easy, attainable, and effective. Every salesperson should buy this book, read it, and memorize it.

The Digital Sales Rep is an absolute must-read for any prospector, salesperson, or networker looking to grow their leads, sales, or career.

Kevin Wilhelm
President, POD Marketing and Marketing4ECPs

Introduction

Imagine closing as many sales in one year as would normally take four. Now imagine doing that during a pandemic when you cannot leave your house.

Well, that is the story of what happened at our marketing agency, Marketing4ECPs, in 2020.

I am a health professional turned salesperson turned entrepreneur and marketer. I'm a speaker, author, business innovator, and growth strategist and just an overall kick-ass, take-names overachiever. Oh, and I also beat stage 4 ovarian cancer!

I started my career in retail optical as a Licensed Optician and quickly moved into corporate training and workforce development, training 150 optical stores how to grow into one of the most profitable chains through sales, marketing, and people management. It was here that I truly saw the power of what sales skills training could do to overall goals and revenue. I was shocked to learn that the majority of employees in sales positions in eye care businesses had zero actual sales training. We would train on sales basics, from proper greetings to lifestyle questioning and closing techniques, which would immediately lead to a minimum of a 25% increase in sales. Now put an incentive program on top of actual skills training and we would see sales and revenue grow by 50% on average. It was astounding.

As that optical chain was being acquired, I was actively being recruited and would take my first role outside healthcare sales with Bausch & Lomb. B&L, as it is known in the industry, is a leading vision care company with three divisions: pharmaceuticals, surgical, and vision care. This new position would challenge me to find new ways to engage, connect, and sell to my target clients in a neglected and saturated territory. I learned some huge sales lessons here that I would take with me to all my future positions and still use today. Don't worry—I am going to share a few in later chapters, so stay tuned. These lessons would also help me win numerous sales awards and bonuses, including Rookie of the Year and Platinum Sales Rep of the Year.

It was at the end of the recession in 2008 when I decided to live the dream and leave my outside sales role. I started my own training and consulting business, which would land me a very lucrative contract position as VP of Training and Marketing for an Optometry group with over 500 members. I would be able to apply my knowledge and expertise in helping small businesses, in this case Optometry practices, grow. I loved seeing small business owners take charge of their businesses by learning about operations, finances, human resources, and, of course, sales and marketing. It always equaled a better-run and more profitable business. It was here that I was truly starting to understand the value of digital marketing and how it can propel growth and revenue in any business.

It was December 2014 when I met my current business partners, Kevin Wilhelm and Karim Ali. They had just started a digital marketing agency focused on the home service sector. They had a dream of creating a niche marketing program focused on a specific industry. I knew this was a gap in the eye care industry, and they had the marketing solution that could truly grow an Optometry practice, so the stars were aligning. I left my vice president role for the unknown, and Marketing4ECPs was born in 2015.

I will share more insights in the following chapters, but let me say this: I was, and still am, the main salesperson growing this company. Every day, it is up to me to make sales happen. The 70+ employees at our office are counting on me to win business. There is no other option but success.

Back to the year of the pandemic ... 2020.

The year had started out strong. We were heading into our fifth year of business. We had worked hard to grow a marketing agency from the ground up. We did everything to gain brand awareness and sell our services, from walking our own talk when it came to marketing our company to trade shows and speaking, and basically networking like there's no tomorrow to connect with our target audience. We had 150 monthly retainer clients thanks to our efforts in the first four years and over $2.5 million in annual revenue.

We were forecasting to have our best year ever at the beginning of 2020. The sales were flowing in at a very steady rate. I was at a conference and trade show in Kansas City, Missouri, when I first heard about COVID-19. It all happened so quickly from that moment on, and within a month we were in lockdown. Not only were we in lockdown but so were all our marketing clients, and many of them were panicking. Within three days of the lockdown, our clients had canceled or paused over $100,000 in monthly recurring revenue or, to put it in perspective, 1,000,000 annual dollars. Yes, we are talking about almost half of our revenue. It was a big hit. Not much scares me, but I was nervous at that point. I was also angry. We had worked so hard and invested so much time and money to get to where we were, only to lose half of it in the blink of an eye (no eye care pun intended:)).

I think the saying "Pressure makes diamonds" fits perfectly here.

When you are faced with a challenge this gigantic, you need to come out swinging. My business partners and I mobilized the team. We knew our response would dictate our outcomes and we needed a plan. First thing we did was drop everything to help our clients communicate to their customers that they were closing. We created social posts, web banners, and email blasts all within twenty-four hours of our clients' closing. We let our clients pause any of their advertising solutions and offered deferrals on monthly subscriptions. Even though it hurt our revenue immensely, we knew if we treated our clients right in times of trouble, they would stay loyal, and we would get their business back once they reopened. Our goodwill has come back to us tenfold. We never lost a client, and we have gained back most of the lost revenue from our existing clients.

 But that was only the beginning of bigger things.

Let us talk about what happened to change the trajectory of our business forever.

We did three things that would gain us more exposure and goodwill in a short period of time and start a chain reaction of our targeted clients reaching out to us.

We developed resources within days of the lockdown that would help our clients with information on how to safeguard their businesses as they were closing. This simple e-book, written out of a desire to help, was downloaded hundreds of times. It was so practical and impactful that other industry suppliers were asking for it to be sent to their clients.

We launched a webinar with optometrist clients as panelists on day six of the lockdown, so those in the industry could hear from their peers about how they were coping with being closed. This would turn into a webinar each week for four months that would see thousands register to attend live and thousands more watching the on-demand recordings. We have one webinar that has been viewed over 56,000 times. Talk about exposure!

We knew prospective new clients were also stuck at home. They were on their computers more than they ever would be again, so we built a digital plan to start reaching out. Using multiple platforms, we connected with more of our targeted clients by being forced to think differently and more digitally than we ever had, using traditional sales avenues like trade shows. I tested and developed the 10 + 10 Sales System.

Previously, it took us four years to close 150 clients, but in 2020, during one of the most challenging years for all businesses, we took on 110 new clients. Most businesses would have been happy just to keep business running during a pandemic, but we blew away sales targets. Any marketing agency will tell you 100+ clients in one year is astounding. The following year, we took on 150 new clients in the first six months.

And there are no signs of slowing down.

I wrote this book to help salespeople in all sectors move to digital selling along with traditional selling. The 10 + 10 Sales System works. At first I thought it might be just me, so I hired a Digital Prospector (my new name for inside salespeople) and taught him my system. He had outside sales experience, but it mostly involved cold-calling and knocking on doors. I showed him the power of reaching out digitally and the sheer volume you can hit in one day on the computer with the right plan. He is crushing it every day!

Ready to crush it yourself? Ready to learn the plan?

CHAPTER 1

The New Sales Road Is Digital

These are times of great change.
Will they crush you or catapult you?

—BRIAN HALLIGAN, CEO | HUBSPOT

I have been in sales for a long time. As a sales rep, prospecting was always a pretty standard affair. You had a few options: knock on doors, pick up the phone, try to book a meeting with the decision maker, go to trade shows and stand at a booth all day, or try to send out a direct mail piece and hope someone calls you.

Things started to change when the internet took over. I was ready when that happened to adapt and embrace the new digital world and was always trying to find new ways to connect with my target client.

But a pandemic would change everything we knew in sales and business. If you had embraced any digital technology before the lockdown, then you would be leaps and bounds ahead of your competitors. If you had not, you had a steep learning curve to understand how to do digital outreach of any kind.

The pandemic has changed sales as we know it. Some of our target clients may never go back to working in an office. Working from home will be the new office. It may take years for trade shows to be a thing again, if ever.

So, clearly, the new sales road is a digital road mixed with the traditional. And I will tell you from firsthand experience, it is a better road. A more productive and lucrative road.

I want to start by saying I am not just writing a book about sales; I live and breathe sales every day. I get up every morning and get ready to do the sales battle. I get excited even just thinking about sales. I admit it. *I am obsessed with sales.*

My morning routine: coffee, check email, prospect, message, set up virtual demos, follow up, repeat.

It is like a sales exercise program and, just like exercise, the more you stick to it, the more results you see. I am very committed to my sales exercise program. It's because it works!

But it wasn't always that way. I wish I had created the 10 + 10 Sales System years ago! But what do they say? Hindsight is 20/20? (Oops, another eye-related pun!)

I think we all wish we had a crystal ball. It would make things so much easier.

Life and business have been like rollercoasters over the years. Some real ups and downs. I am not one to rehash the worst times in my life, but life has liked to challenge me. I lost both my parents in my thirties. I lost a brother a few years ago, and I was diagnosed with stage 4 ovarian cancer in 2016, less than a year after starting my business. The cancer was a tough one that really made me revisit my life and accomplishments. It is why I continue to strive to be the best. I feel an obligation to a higher power that allows me to live every day, and to not waste it. Some of those hardest times in my life were the ones that brought about the most amazing changes and pivotal moments that would change my life trajectory. Repeatedly, something in my life would change my direction. It got to a point that when something challenging would happen, I would already start to look for the lesson or the "sign" of what it was supposed to mean or what I should do.

I remember one of those first signs like it was yesterday.

I was working as an optician and manager of a huge one-hour optical store. I was feeling very underchallenged in the role I was in. I had been there a long time and felt a bit, well, stuck. I was sent to a customer service workshop and, as I listened to the presenter, I literally sat up in my chair and said to myself, *This is what I want to do.* She was inspiring and enlightening, and her message was so impactful. It was a very clear sign. I knew at that moment I wanted to do public speaking. I went back home and set things in motion. You will learn as you read that I am a doer, so when I get an idea, I start putting it into action.

I set up a meeting with my supervisor and told her my vision of speaking and training for our company. I was scared. I had no idea how she or the optical chain owners would respond to my request. The good news is they had already been considering the idea before I brought it to them, and within a short period of time I became a Corporate Trainer for 170 stores—designing, delivering, and facilitating training programs on everything from management to … you guessed it, **sales**. You might have heard the stat before that people fear public speaking more than death, according to a 1973 study of American Fears by R. H. Bruskin Associates.[1] I will tell you, those first few times I got up in front of a group of people to deliver a workshop on sales skills were some of the scariest moments of my life, but also the most exhilarating.

I was doing what I was meant to do.

---

[1] Peter Watson, "What People Usually Fear" (London: *The Sunday Times*, 1973), 9.

That same presenter, Barbara Mills, who became my mentor, also said some things I have used to motivate myself all of these years. She said, "Everything you want is just one step over fear." She also said, "You need to get uncomfortable in your present situation to move forward and grow."

If there was ever a year to test you and your comfort zones, it would be the year of the pandemic.

The year 2020 was one of challenges for most businesses. It was a time we were all uncomfortable and you either rose to the challenge or you withered. It was a year when you had to do everything differently, learn new ways of communication, set up your workforce to work from home, and, in my case, still do sales. Who is going to buy during a pandemic?

Here is what it looked like: I am in lockdown and forced to work from home.

My target client's businesses are closed due to the lockdown. They are stuck at home. Trade shows are canceled. Speaking events are canceled. Cold calling is out of the question because all we have are the work numbers and our prospects are at home.

How am I going to do sales? I knew at that moment I had to look for new ways to reach out, connect, and get leads.

Listen, I am not new to digital platforms. I own a digital marketing company. I am also not new to digital prospecting, but I never had to rely on it. In fact, because I had never focused on it I really did not know what I could produce digitally. I realized I had to get invested in digital prospecting, to build a system of outreach so that I could track everything from how much outreach to what was working, and what was driving connections and results. What would get me a live (well, virtual live) demo?

I needed to build a plan.

I like organization. I like tracking (mostly because I do not have a twenty-year-old's memory anymore, but also for quick review of outreach and follow-up). I like check marks. (That means a sale: ✓.) I like social media. And I also like to teach others.

To build the plan and the tracking, I also needed to answer some questions:

- Who is my target audience?
- What territory is my target audience in?
- Where is my target audience spending time (digitally)?
- What is important to them at this particular time?
- Are there any industry partners out there who could help me with connecting to my target audience?
- What could I create that would make someone connect with me or give me their contact information?

Once I had answered the questions above, I really needed to look at my target clients and later identify what was different about them post-pandemic.

 The new B2B client:

- Remote
- Connected
- Social
- Virtual
- Juggling multiple tasks

My target clients are very different from what they used to be. They used to be more carefree, had very few business challenges, and often worked a three- or four-day work week. Now they are busy, being forced to space out appointments and ensure cleaning protocols that limit the number of patients they can see. They are also trying to navigate a new normal: running a business during a pandemic, keeping staff motivated and safe, and making up for the losses of being closed for three months while not being able to see as many appointments. So, when it comes to us trying to connect with them, they say they want to hear from vendors and salespeople, but their expectations are very different. They do not want a face-to-face meeting anymore. They have learned that they can save time by seeing you remotely. Time, to most of them, means money. And safety. They are willing to invite you virtually into their homes for sales presentations, so learning how to deliver an amazing virtual sales experience is a crucial business strategy for today and for the future.

Here is what buyers will expect from you, their digital salesperson:

- Technology enabled
- Well-planned virtual demonstration
- Social presence and activity
- Always online—always available
- Multiple ways to connect (email, website, cell, text, social)
- Online expert
- Familiar with all virtual platforms

I do not think sales are ever going back to the way they were before. Maybe nothing is really going to go back to the way it was before the pandemic. Think about it this way: We have taught everyone that they can work from home, including our clients. A lot of our buyers or target clients are going to stay working from home for the foreseeable future. This is not something that will end when we are out of the current situation. This will be an ongoing change. They are also now happy with virtual meetings and will continue to be open to meeting remotely. You will need to be able to find, attract, connect with, and present to a buyer digitally. I am going to show you how.

Gone are the majority of onsite meetings and in-person sales demonstrations. Trade shows will return, but they won't be what they used to be. Hello to virtual everything! Buyers are getting used to this type of sales experience and liking it!

Gone are the days of cold calling. Sales reps hate cold calling anyway, but listen—there's a better way!

Salespeople are also seeing advantages to learning how to digitally prospect and connect. You can be way more efficient working from your home office. I know I am! First, I am going to show you how to connect with up to one hundred target clients a day. There's no way you can do that on the road unless you are at a trade show, and even then it's tough to get to one hundred qualified prospects.

Then I am going to show you what to do once they connect back.

Stop getting on a plane or in a car and start getting digital. Or if you are back on the road, mix traditional with digital.

The Old Selling	The New Selling
In person	Remote
On the phone	On email
Travel site visits	Video conferencing
Live demonstrations	Webinars
Trade show	Virtual conferences and virtual booths
Connecting at an event	Connecting on social media

I see a different future for buying and selling. I have lived it and thrived in it. It will be fast, agile, ever-changing, more technology-oriented, focused on online platforms, and demanding. If you learn the nuances of prospecting, connecting, engaging, and presenting online, you will win a lot of business.

Move to become a Digital Sales Rep!

So, let us talk about what you need to master to become a digital sales rep.

If you are a millennial, you grew up with technology, so this is going to be easier for you. Millennials make up 50% of the workforce these days, so they are the new salespeople, but they are also our new buyers. If you are not a millennial ... no worries. It is super easy, and I am going to walk you through this program.

I will be honest, I absolutely LOVE selling digitally. It has been more than effective for my results. I can talk to a client in California one hour and then one in Toronto the next hour. I have trained myself on every virtual platform available and have fine-tuned an online demonstration of my products and services to a point where it is second nature to recite it.

Where you should start on your road to becoming a digital sales rep:

1. Digital expert:

Do not wait for your organization to make you a digital sales expert. No one taught me how to use LinkedIn or how to craft the perfect email. I looked for training on LinkedIn, YouTube, Udemy, and Google and spent all of my free time learning the ins and outs of building a presence on LinkedIn and how to connect with my target client. Invest your time in learning; it will come back to you in sales. There is a ton of free information out there.

2. Digital channels:

There are a lot of different digital channels you can use for sales efforts. My advice is to start with a couple and master them before moving on to others. It is better to be great at a few than not so great at many. The four channels I use every day are email, LinkedIn, Instagram, and Facebook. I see other sales reps use channels like Pinterest, TikTok, Clubhouse, and Alignable, to name a few, and I am on every one of those as well, but I get the best results on the four I am going to teach you about in this book.

3. Digital presence:

The first exercise is to set up an account on these platforms, if you have not already done so, and build a great profile on each one. I will give you exact examples of what you need to do in each dedicated chapter. I also want you to find some sales reps in your industry to follow who are doing what we teach here and crushing it on these platforms. They use these social channels for business, not for personal. In fact, the salespeople who are most effective rarely post personal posts. It is all business. Start by following me! I post almost every day. Look at how I set my profiles up, copy anything you like, and watch what I post. Think about how you can use that inspiration to create the posts you will share.

- **LinkedIn**: https://www.linkedin.com/in/trudicharest/
- **Instagram**: https://www.instagram.com/digitalsalesrep/ *and* https://www.instagram.com/eyecaremarketer/
- **Facebook**: https://www.facebook.com/groups/digitalsalesrep

4. Digital outreach:

Building an outreach strategy is a numbers game. The more you reach out and try to connect with your target audience, the more you will see them connect back. I never get upset if someone does not connect with me immediately. I often see people connect months later or, in a few cases, years later. I am going to show you exactly what I do on each of these platforms and channels to connect, but start thinking about what you would email or message to a potential client who has engaged with you. Also, consider what you will post every day that captures attention and interest and is not all about sales and self-promotion.

Homework: Put all of these in a file:

- Create two email scripts you would send to a potential client.

- Create a short, three- to four-sentence message you would send someone on LinkedIn.

- Have two or three social posts ready to use that would engage your target audience.

(Need some inspiration? Go to my website www.thedigitalsalesrep.com and download the FREE file under resources with my favorite email templates and LinkedIn message scripts.)

5. Digital relationships:

Commit to building digital relationships through sharing valuable information. My secret has not been in connecting and hitting clients up with immediate sales messages. In fact, I HATE it when salespeople spam me. I have given you my connection freely, so now use my time and visibility wisely. Do not send me automated messages that are not at all personal or engaging. I do not want to meet with you seconds after connecting with you. I want to get to know you and have you get to know me. My secret has been in my digital relationship-building. I share engaging, relevant industry content. I use the philosophy of giving something before you ask for something. If I do reach out to introduce myself and my company, I give something free as well. And I use my "no-pressure sales tactics" that you will learn in Chapter 3. This is why no one ever unfollows me. Stay tuned for more on that.

6. Digital tools:

There are a ton of digital tools and technology to help in your sales outreach efforts. I use technology to create social posts, schedule and plan social posts, create e-books and presentations, host webinars and virtual meetings, email my database, track sales outreach, and so much more! There are too many to list here, so I have made a page on my website that has links to every single tool in my arsenal and a few extra! Go to www.thedigitalsalesrep.com and click on the resources tab.

I am seriously excited about this new digital sales world. I am thankful every day for the abundance of digital tools available to find and close sales leads. I use all of my previous sales skills, but now I use them online. I am grateful that there was a time that someone pushed me out of my comfort zone, because I have been pushing myself ever since.

Remember—everything you want is just one step over fear.

I will help you. Let us take that step together.

I read this quote while doing research for this book:

Ninety percent of CEOs believe the digital economy will impact their industry, but less than 15% are executing on a digital strategy.

—MIT Sloan Management Review and Capgemini Consulting

Even in my own industry I see only a handful of salespeople doing any digital prospecting or social selling. It is not optional any longer; it's essential.

Hot Points to Remember:

- Buyers want the option of a virtual meeting
- Only you can make yourself a digital expert
- Building a digital presence is your new sales strategy

✓ CHAPTER 1 TO-DO LIST

Who is my target audience? In my case, it is eye care professionals who own their own businesses, or clinics, optometrists, opticians, and ophthalmologists. Maybe you sell Botox and aesthetic supplies, so your target audience is spas, salons, estheticians, dermatologists, and other licensed practitioners. Write down everyone who could be a target client.

Make a complete list of contacts you already have. You may even have a list from your current organization. Do not rely just on this list; it often is not actively updated with new opportunities and businesses that have just opened. Think outside the box. Can you add to your target list? Is there a sector you have not focused on? For example, when I first started prospecting for marketing clients, I started with optometrists who owned their own stand-alone practices. What I missed for quite a few years were optometrists who owned or subleased the spaces next door to large chains like LensCrafters. In fact, they need marketing even more than other practices because they have fewer revenue opportunities. They needed to fill their schedules. Start to build your list.

What territory is my target audience in? I am lucky in the fact that my target audience could be global, but for now we concentrate on North America. Your target territory may be even smaller, like one state or province. Your big homework exercise here is to find every one of your target clients in your territory. As we mentioned above, you may have a list from your current company. Are there targets you can add to the list? How do you find them in your territory? Try Google, industry directories, association databases, group lists, and job sites.

Where is my target audience spending time? Obviously, this is super important because I want to spend my prospecting time effectively, so I want to be where my target client is. Are they on LinkedIn, Instagram, Facebook, webinars, groups, forums, community chat groups, Clubhouse, TikTok, or where? The list goes on. Do your own investigation. I reached out and asked a few of my current clients where they spend time socially and digitally to understand the platforms that will work best to prospect. You need to find out what will work for your industry.

What is important to them at this particular time? Why is this question so relevant? To be great at sales, you need to be great at understanding your customer's business. You might be selling them toothbrushes and toothpaste or new teeth-whitening equipment, but their main challenge right now is finding staff. If they do not have enough staff, bringing on a new piece of equipment is likely not in the cards until they fix their human resources issues. Learn their challenges and what is happening to them at this time, and you will see opportunities to help them. I have made many sales by reaching out and helping a client with some resources or advice. I use a motto daily: Solve to sell. Help them solve their issues, and they will buy from you.

Are there any industry partnerships out there that could connect me with my target audience? Have you heard the saying "We are stronger together than apart"? Same goes for sales. Every industry has an opportunity for you to go and find ways to partner with other sales reps to refer to each other or to groups where you can speak to their networks or even to noncompeting companies to find ways to give each other exposure to their networks. Think of two partnerships that you could create that would give you some immediate connections that you might not easily obtain on your own.

What could I create that would make someone connect with me or give me their contact information? I am a marketer, so lead magnets are my thing. I create e-books, checklists, e-guides, templates, scripts, and files of resources that my target audience wants. Then I offer it all to them in my outreach—but I ask them to opt into my email program to download them.

CHAPTER 2

Think Like a Marketer

The best marketing doesn't feel like marketing.

—TOM FISHBURNE

I know it's cheesy, but I LOVE the TV shows *The Bachelor* and *The Bachelorette*.

They always hook me right at the beginning when they play the intro trailers and say things like, "This is going to be the most dramatic rose season ever," or "… an ending like you have never seen before on *The Bachelor*."

I have to watch it. It's like an addiction. Even though most of the time it is pretty predictable, I still want to see the engagement proposal at the end. The franchise knows that #BachelorNation fans like some of the traditional segments of the show, like the cocktail parties and rose ceremonies, but it has also kept us on our toes with a few changes like starting a season with two Bachelorettes instead of one, or introducing five new ladies into the house four weeks into the season. It is just smart marketing to keep things simple but change a few things up at the same time. It's likely they were doing a little social listening to hear what fans were saying they loved or hated about the current season.

As we grow you into a powerful digital sales rep, it starts with knowing what to do and not do online. It is also about standing out and being bold enough, so your target audience starts to take notice.

$ Sales have always been about getting and keeping attention. Using marketing tactics to get in front of your customers and have them connect with you is a smart sales strategy. Today's digital sales rep needs to be part marketer, part social media guru, part digital expert, part copywriter, part graphic designer, and, of course, part salesperson.

What are some **sales and marketing** takeaways from watching *The Bachelor*?

1. **First impressions matter:**

Especially making an impression digitally when you only have seconds to capture someone's attention. Whether it is a social post or an email, make sure it is worthy of sending out to your audience. You might never get another chance to make an impression.

2. **Be memorable:**

I always laugh at what some of the guests do the first night to stand out. From crazy costumes to arriving in fancy vehicles, they are looking to grab some attention that will make the Bachelor or Bachelorette remember them. What can you do that is fun, memorable, and different?

3. **Don't be shy:**

For guests, there's very little time with the Bachelor or Bachelorette, so obviously time is of great value. Those who make things happen to grab available time and be memorable usually stay longer in the Bachelor house. It's the same online. It's the people who are posting great content, sharing relevant resources, and staying super visible who are the ones who are remembered, and their networks grow because of it.

4. Stay out of trouble:

There is always someone on the show creating chaos or tension. I can't believe I am saying this, but it needs to be said: I have seen my share of people, including industry sales reps, who voice a little too much online. Don't gossip, post negative comments, lie, like posts if you don't want others to see you liked them, or post political beliefs or anything that can be considered offensive. Just think before you post.

5. Be authentic:

Be yourself. Create an online presence that is true to yourself, but also professional and sales worthy. Find something that makes you unique and is a reason your target audience will want to connect with you. Think of what you are truly good at and bring that into your online sales and marketing every day.

6. Know your limit:

If you watch *The Bachelor,* there is always one person who overindulges on alcohol the first night. There are also people who overindulge online. Don't get into people's personal digital space too often. There is a time and place for social posting, sharing, commenting, and liking. When you do it right, your target audience will appreciate it and embrace it. If you do it wrong, or too much, they will unfollow or, worse, block you.

OK, enough about *The Bachelor.* Let's talk about digital marketing.

If you are with a large organization, you probably have a full sales division and marketing department. This department is busy creating sales brochures and trade show booths but also all things digital, like the company website, blogs, social media, e-commerce, email marketing, videos, digital ads, and magazine ads.

Unfortunately, there is one thing that I have personally experienced, as well as seen, across healthcare industries. It is that marketing rarely teaches sales how to use the amazing marketing assets they are creating.

Before I owned a marketing company, I worked for a large pharmaceutical company that had a substantially smaller marketing team. Therefore, we had to come up with a lot of our own sales tools, ideas, and initiatives. To some of you, the thought of trying to create content is overwhelming. Don't worry. We will give you some great ideas on how to create your own marketing materials easily and effortlessly.

Let's start with utilizing marketing from your current company. I will use my company, Marketing4ECPs, as an example of how I utilize their assets and resources in my personal posting and outreach strategy.

Blogs

We produce two marketing blogs a month. As soon as they are published, I copy the link (URL) of the blog post and the image (I use Snipping Tool to grab the image) and I post them to all of my social channels, including LinkedIn, Instagram, Facebook, and Pinterest.

Trudi Charest
Co-Founder at 4ECPs I Speaker I Marketer I Eye Care Business Strategist I Influen...
5d • Edited •

I spend a lot of time on LinkedIn. At least an hour a day! Most of my current and prospective clients are on here (Optometrists, Opticians, etc.) so I often am on their personal and business pages. I only see a handful taking advantage of th ...see more

Why You Need a Personal Profile on LinkedIn to Help Your Eye Care Business

Posted on April 1, 2021 by Trudi Charest

19 • 1 comment

Webinars

We host a monthly webinar. I obtain the social post and link to register for the webinar and post it to my social channels. Although I am driving registration and traffic to my company webinar, my followers find this super helpful and appreciate the invitations to our webinars.

e-Books and Resources

We not only write some great informational e-books, but we also create valuable downloads, like files full of social posts and self-audit forms. Whenever there is something new posted to our website, I ask for the images from our marketing team, or copy them from the website along with the link (URL), and post them to all of my social channels.

Newsletters and Email Blasts

We send a bi-weekly email blast to our email subscribers. I will also watch what our internal marketing team is communicating in the email and either post it to my social media or forward the email to select prospects or clients who might be interested.

Image Bank

I have a file of marketing posts that I can use over and over again on social media when I need a call to action—like booking a meeting with me, or checking out our recent work—or to highlight what we do. I post to my social following and drive them back to my personal email or company website to book a meeting with me. Think what marketing assets, but also product images, you can use to build your own posts.

Follow Your Company's Social Channels and Like or Share

This is absolutely the easiest way to get access to your company's marketing materials and posts. Follow them on LinkedIn, Instagram, Facebook, Pinterest, Twitter, and any other social platform they are on. Then start sharing and liking.

Some of the best sales reps who are crushing it on social media make their own posts, such as:

Social Posts

Take pictures with your mobile phone of your product or service and of some of your current customers and experiences. These personal posts often get way better engagement and traction than the standard company marketing posts, but learn how to do it right. Take the time to learn better photography techniques, as well as editing and adding text. Video also works amazingly well, but it is also a bit of learning curve and takes some skill to get it right. There are a ton of tutorials online and amazing editing apps that can help you.

Social Stories

Stories and reels are all the rage on Instagram, Facebook, and now LinkedIn. This a great way to use your mobile phone to capture some great video or images of your product or service and showcase it in a fun storyboard.

Make Social Posts

I use Canva to make social media posts and stories. I even use it to make email blasts, presentations, social media covers for LinkedIn and Facebook, and so much more. Canva is truly a serious asset to making digital marketing materials quickly and without a graphic designer. There is a FREE and PRO version, so try it out and see what you can create.

Email

I ask all my contacts, clients, and followers if I can add them to my personal (not company) email database. I let them know I will keep them updated on new products, offerings, and programs that we have, as well as invite them to special events we are hosting. I rarely get a rejection. When you ask for their email, let them know the value of what you will be sending them. Then I create my own email scripts and graphics to send out. I also try to think of catchy headlines or subject lines to get the receiver to open my email. I do not make them sales-oriented at all because they might also get flagged as spam. I do headlines like:

- You Don't Want to Miss This …

- Limited Time to Learn More About …

- Important News About …

e-Books

This is a bit more work but worth every bit of time and effort if you build one that answers a challenge your prospective clients are facing right now. For example, my clients were experiencing a tremendous issue with finding good staff. I put together a ten-page e-guide on how to hire better, faster, and more effectively in my industry. I have used it repeatedly for years. You can create your own e-books in Canva or also on a platform called Designrr.

At the end of the day, think about the tactics marketers use to get you to look at a social post and click on it to read further or open an email. What makes you so engaged that you do those actions? Start thinking of how you can do that with your audience.

Your goal is to be visible and engaging. You will subliminally build a relationship with your followers as they see you more and more digitally, as well as socially, and as they like what they are seeing. I have prospective clients tell me that they see me all the time, that they LOVE my Instagram feed, and that they LOVE what I share on LinkedIn because it is so relevant to them and the current challenges and situation. I always think about my target audience and what they would perceive as valuable.

 Hot Points to Remember:

- **Make a great impression online**
- **Visibility will be your key to digital success**
- **Create something unique that will get a ton of engagement**

 **CHAPTER 2 TO-DO LIST**

	Gather resources from your company: images, social posts, ads, and resources.
	Follow all of your company platforms: social media (LinkedIn, Facebook, Instagram, Twitter, Pinterest, TikTok, YouTube, and so on), company pages, website, blogs, webinars, newsletter, and email blasts.
	Sign up for Canva. Sign up for the FREE account and start creating.
	Practice making videos and taking pictures. Use your mobile phone to take a few static pictures of your current product or service, and also try your hand at a video or two. Go to the App Store and download a free app to edit pictures and video.

CHAPTER 3

No-Pressure Sales Tactics That Convert

Give value. Give value. Give value.
And then ask for the business.

—GARY VEE

Life is a series of lessons ... so is sales. If you are not learning and improving, you're losing. I had one of those career-altering sales lessons that would completely change the way I would sell forever.

I had just finished two weeks of sales training with a pharma company and was about to hit the road for my first outside sales job. They taught me a lot of different sales skills and shared some statistics like this one: that 80% of my current business comes from the top 20% of my accounts. And that to concentrate on these top accounts was my first objective. I was told to book lunch with my top ten clients.

My first lunch was with a large downtown Optometry practice with five optometrists and a busy, busy schedule. I arrived early and introduced myself to the receptionist. She told me to have a seat. I waited, and waited, and waited. She finally came over to tell me that the optometrist I was meeting with that day was running late with a patient. I ended up only having five minutes with the practice owner before he needed to go to his next patient.

Lesson #1: Be prepared to present in only five minutes and still give value.

Lesson #2: Always put more money in the parking meter than anticipated.

🍴 My second lunch was with another practice in a suburban setting. This time the doctor was finished with his patients and ready to go to lunch. I was excited and nervous. We sat down and I made some small talk while we ordered our food. As soon as the waiter took the order, I did what I was taught in my sales training and I said, "Doctor, can you tell me about your practice and business?" I was not expecting the reaction I was about to get. The look on his face was pure anger and he threw his fork down. He looked straight at me.

"If I have to teach one more rep about my business I am going to scream. I am about to give you the advice of your career," he said. "I want you to come in here and tell me about my business, not the other way around. Tell me how I am doing with your products; tell me what's happening with other offices and how mine stacks up. Tell me something that is happening that relates to your products. There is only one sales rep who I enjoy having lunch with, and I have lunch with him almost every month. Why? Because it's worth my time. He teaches me something new every time I meet with him. He is an industry expert. He knows everything that is happening. He shows me what I need to do in my practice. He is a resource and I appreciate that. The next time you book lunch with me, make sure it's going to be valuable or don't waste my time."

Damn …

I was only on day two of sales calls in my territory at this point. I felt like crawling into a corner and hiding, but I didn't. In fact, I thought long and hard about what he said and decided to take his advice. I was going to become a resource.

Lesson #3: Be a resource.

I start paying attention to everything I am seeing when I am in client offices.

I am now two weeks into the new sales role. I am getting a clearer picture of my territory as well as the challenges I was going to face being in sales with this company.

Challenge 1: There are four major players in my space, and I am quickly learning I am currently the fourth of four when it comes to industry market share.

Challenge 2: My products at that time were known as the most uncomfortable and the priciest—not an easy thing to sell.

Challenge 3: The company had a major product recall the past year, from which they were still experiencing residual declining sales effects.

Challenge 4: The territory had been neglected and under-serviced for some time.

I realized if I was going to succeed at this job, I would need to figure out how to sell differently. I had to become a trusted advisor—someone people wanted to have lunch with!

I started by going back to the sales and business basics. I knew there were three ways to grow any business, including my territory sales:

- Get more customers

- Get customers to spend more money

- Get customers to come back more often or spend more frequently

I started with number one because I knew if I could get more customers, it would be easier to grow all three from there. How could I get more customers? I decided the first thing I was going to do was knock on every door of potential clients and introduce myself. The sales territory had seen a few new reps over the years and had been sadly neglected. Some clients told me that they had not heard from a rep at my company for more than five years. I went into every single office and dropped off my business card and asked for a meeting. I had a lot of rejections, but I also had some notable successes. **Just the act of showing up** earned me some new accounts that I would grow into sizable revenue generators.

I also needed a hook! Something that none of my competitors were offering that would get me in front of decision makers. I decided to ask my top accounts what their main business challenges were. I was shocked at how almost all the accounts' answers listed the same issues:

- Finding good staff
- Training staff
- Finding time to make improvements to the business

I immediately knew I could help with all three. I spent the next weekend writing a ten-page e-guide on how to hire better, including resources on where and how to post jobs in the eye care industry. I made an electronic copy and printed copies and gave it out to all my accounts. Instantly, I was a **resource**.

Next, I spent some time creating a training presentation. I could offer my accounts a lunch-and-learn program. I wanted something that would entice the practice owner (and buyer of my products) to be present. I wanted to ensure the training would be helpful for the practice but also assist in driving sales of my products. I created a basic presentation on

"How to Answer the Phone" that included how to answer the top questions every eye care practice is asked on the phone. One of those questions just happened to be about contact lenses, which is what I sold. In my first year, I did over fifty lunch-and-learn presentations and was gaining amazing exposure to my target client. And, by the way, **sales were growing steadily**.

I looked at the third challenge and came up with a way I could save practices time and grow business. Every time I was in a practice or optical store, there were two things I noticed I could help with. The first one was filling up their trial contact lens kits that they used to fit new patients, and the second was to take any credits they had and ship them back to the head office for return—two extremely tedious tasks that practice staff hated doing and therefore were often neglected. By filling the trial kits, I immediately saw sales go up. If the trials they were looking for were available, my product was fit by the doctor more often. By taking care of the returns, I earned goodwill with the staff, and that assisted in booking appointments with the decision makers more easily. When you do something for staff at an office, they remember.

My goal of becoming a resource was working. I was gaining traction and growing sales in accounts all over my territory. In my first year at this company, I grew my overall sales revenue by 27% and won Rookie of the Year.

I didn't grow sales by selling; I grew sales by helping.

It's amazing how people want to give you business when they like and appreciate you.

Give, give, give, ask—that became my motto. Be helpful; be a resource. Show up. Make sure everyone knows you. Those were my objectives that year and they paid off. Even my competitors were asking, "What the hell is going on?"

What can you take from this story? Ask your top clients what their challenges are. Brainstorm what you can create to help with those challenges. Do what your competitors are not willing to do.

Those were the days when sales reps were mandated to see five appointments a day, five days a week. It was all about being on the road, driving and driving from appointment to appointment. There was very little time in the home office, and I typically did admin work from my car while waiting for the next appointment. It's amazing when I think about it because it is so ineffective in comparison to the volume of clients I can touch in a day virtually now.

That leads me to digital prospecting.

Let me tell one of my first experiences with digital outreach and prospecting.

I had just returned from a regional meeting with my direct supervisor, Kim Pearce, and the other sales representatives in the west. I am like a sponge at these events because there is a wealth of sales experience sitting at that table. It was at this meeting where one of the reps talked about how she had to be at home for a few days the previous week but that she used the time effectively and "dialed for dollars." She said she called her top accounts and asked them if she could top up some of the supplies and ended up with four times the orders she would have received—by driving to each account. I was intrigued. The next day, this story would catapult my sales to levels only imagined.

I actually heard it on the news before I heard it from our team. One of our competitors had just had a major recall of one of their products. I knew this would substantially affect all my accounts. I started that day by going to my scheduled appointments and saw the chaos the recall was causing, and I immediately saw an opportunity to help. I offered some of our trial products for free that they could use to replace the recalled products, but I also asked the practices if they wanted to buy the retail sizes. They all said yes. They were extremely grateful for the free product and happy to order a full retail-priced product. I went home at the end of that day, canceled all my appointments for the following two days, and got on the phone. I called every one of my accounts, and a few I had never made inroads with, and did the same thing. I offered them some free trial products and asked if they wanted to buy. Not everyone bought, but almost everyone took me up on the free products. I called over 400 accounts in two days, and that retail product alone I sold 200% more of than had ever been sold in that territory. I would end that year with a 108% increase in overall sales revenue and the coveted award of Platinum Rep of the Year.

 All out of a desire to help.

So, how do I use the philosophies I successfully applied in traditional sales roles to now connect and prospect a completely unknown potential client online? How could I be a resource online? How could I help prospects online? It's one thing to find a prospect's profile on a social channel and another to convince them to receive a connection and direct messages. There were three things I would pull from my traditional sales experience that would help me with digital prospecting:

- People like to connect with expert, resourceful people in their industry
- People love FREE valuable resources
- People don't like to be sold to, but they do like to be helped

Now to build a Digital Outreach Strategy. I'll break outreach into two parts: organic outreach and direct outreach.

1. Organic Outreach:

The first step in building an organic outreach strategy is defining where to reach out. It is like fishing. Some spots are better than others. Specific fish are in specific waters. Some require a certain type of bait. But at the end of the day, the wider the net you cast, the more opportunity you will have. Prospecting is no different—**it's a numbers game.** The more you reach out, the more you will have the opportunity to catch something. If there is one thing I know about fishing, it is that you will catch nothing if you don't put a line in the water.

Just like fishing, there will be challenges. Some fish will swim right past your bait without noticing it. Some fish see the bait and actively swim the other way. Some will bite the hook, only to be lost while you're bringing them in. It will take patience and perseverance. There will be days when you catch zero. If it were easy, everyone would be fishing. The joy is often in the entire experience, and of course the best part is when you actively catch something.

 Where to reach out? **Go to where the fish are.**

I have tested (and still test) every digital option available for prospecting. When Clubhouse was in beta testing, I was there checking out the platform and learning the nuances so I could see if it would work for outreach. The consensus is still out on that one. But what I have found that get me results are the following:

- Email
- LinkedIn
- Instagram
- Facebook

Because it is time-consuming to do prospecting well on any channel, I stick to these four, with a little effort here and there on other platforms. LinkedIn is my personal favorite, but I continue to close business from all four platforms every single week.

I describe organic outreach as what I am posting and sharing without any paid advertising involvement. The first part of the organic outreach is the actual profile setup. A great profile on LinkedIn, Facebook, or Instagram is paramount to getting people interested when they land on your page.

From the profile picture to the position title, make sure you are interesting and fresh.

Go to my LinkedIn profile at https://www.linkedin.com/in/trudicharest/ and read each section. Now go to your profile and rewrite everything to make it sound more professional, robust, exciting, and interesting.

After you are set up with a great profile, you'll want to start thinking about your content strategy. We chatted in the last chapter about ideas on posting and sharing, so now start putting that into play. I dive into exact strategies for outreach on each of these channels in their individual chapters, but I also look at efficiencies. Can you share the same thing on LinkedIn, Instagram, and Facebook? Of course you can! In fact, reuse your content whenever you can. It is OK if someone is following you on all channels. Repetition makes your message more powerful and memorable.

Organic outreach is helping you build a following and a reputation. It is setting you up as an expert in the industry. It allows you to form relationships with your connections and hopefully their followers. The more your following likes, shares, and comments on your posts, the more your target audience will see it. The more you post and share, the more you will see clients reaching out to you to connect with them. On Instagram I average five new followers a day, solely based on my posts. That's twenty-five new prospects a week.

2. **Direct Outreach:**

Direct outreach is exactly what it sounds like—a direct follow or a request to connect from you, not an automated bot. And once connected it includes direct messaging. This is easily how I have grown my network by 50% and sales by over 20% year over year for the last five years.

Some people relate direct outreach online to cold calling, only digital. I personally think it is much more like online dating. Yes, really! :)

Online dating is about research, preparation, cold outreach, communication, and wooing. You can find the profile of a person you would like to date, but you must find a way to get them to want to date you, too! These exact same actions are required for prospecting outreach.

I get it—direct outreach can be scary. It is sort of like cold calling or door knocking, which, let's face it, almost every salesperson on Earth hates. I also see a lot of spammy outreach as I get it myself every day. Someone asks me to connect and then they send me a bunch of automated messages. Well, that is not what I am talking about here. Your direct outreach should follow the philosophy of this entire chapter. Give, give, give, ask! And not automated!

If they see you as an industry expert, if they see their colleagues are connected to you and liking your posts, if they feel it will be of value to connect with you, they will. Then you need to make sure it is valuable.

When I am reaching out and asking people to connect on LinkedIn, as an example, I write a personal direct message:

> *Hi Dr. Smith. I am reaching out, as I would like to add you to my network. I promise to share some amazing eye care marketing tips, resources, and examples that will help you grow your practice.*

I try to be different from the zillion marketing agencies that are reaching out to them. I try to keep my messaging and resources super relevant to the industry and their business. I also know there will be a lot of rejection and deleted requests. That's OK. I look at it as a part of marketing. They may not connect back, but they likely saw the request, may have even looked at my profile, and for a brief instance they saw my name and my company name. So, I don't look at it like a rejection. I consider it exposure. And the more exposure I can get, the better.

AHA Moment: *Don't be like the rest of them, darling!*—Coco Channel

Most salespeople who are prospecting digitally set up automated messages that sound automated and salesy. Do not try to sell to your prospects until they get to know you. Even though I am a marketing company, I do very little automation when it comes to prospecting.

 Hot Points to Remember:

- **Give, give, give, ask**
- **Be prepared to present virtually anywhere, anytime for five minutes or five hours**
- **Digital prospecting is just like dating—you must make someone want to date you back**

✓ CHAPTER 3 TO-DO LIST

	Set up profiles if you do not already have them on LinkedIn, Instagram, and Facebook.
	Check to see what email platform your company uses for automated emails. Start to build a personal database of every current client and every potential client and add in their email addresses. Also add their LinkedIn profile links, Facebook, and Instagram links. If you feel comfortable, start following them and ask them to connect with you.
	Go to your top ten clients and ask them to list their main business challenges.

CHAPTER 4

What Is the 10 + 10 Sales System?

You don't rise to the level of your goals; you fall to the level of your systems.

—RICH WILKERSON

If you ask any of my siblings, our favorite childhood memories are of our summer vacations. My parents would pack up the five kids in the station wagon and head out to Vancouver Island to visit my uncle and his family. It was the journey there and back that created most of the truly memorable moments. The drive through the mountains had lots of amazing places to stop and do all sorts of tourist activities.

We would often stop at creek beds and rocky streams along the way, so we kids could get out of the car and use up some energy. But it was also so my father could do his favorite vacation activity, gold panning. His favorite saying during those trips was, "There's gold in them there mountains." He was determined to find some of it. My father was always a gambler of sorts. Where some wasted their money on lottery tickets, my father could be found spending his time hunting for gold. He found a few specks of gold over the years, nothing of any consequence, but those were some of the times I saw him the most relaxed and happy.

My father was always teaching us kids about the value of hard work. He had to drop out of school and start working in the optical business at sixteen to help support his family. Not only was he one of the hardest working people I have ever known, but he was also the most positive and optimistic. He always saw the bright side of everything in life. He had a motto he would use in life and business, "You won't find what you don't go looking for or work for." He taught us that what we want is out there and often right in front of us. We must go after it.

Which is why his gold-panning aspirations seemed in alignment with his business values.

The principle around gold panning is simple: gold is heavier than the sand and gravel, so once you sift it in the pan, the gold will be left after the other particles leave the pan. However, my father did not rely on luck. Hunting for gold wasn't without a system. You need the right equipment and tools, as well as an idea of what mountain stream and area to pan. **You need a plan, a direction, and a system!** That's right, a system. Most things that are done well start with a process and a system.

Striking Gold with the 10 + 10 Sales System!

As I was building my outreach prospecting strategy, I was all over the place. I had no plan or system in place. I was testing out all the different digital options for outreach without really any tracking of efforts or results. I needed to create a way to **see** all my outreach at a glance. Although I was using Pipedrive, a sales- and leads-based platform, to upload any demos or actual sales presentations, I was not tracking additional outreach efforts. Tracking would become crucial to not only my follow-up strategies but also to quickly seeing where there were opportunities to reach out again.

I started a simple Excel spreadsheet to create the master outreach database, but know you can use any CRM that you are currently using if it works well for you. I created all the headings and tabs for the information I wanted to collect. Here is what I was going to add to the master prospecting database:

- Business name
- Address, city, state
- Owner and decision maker name
- Email address
- Where I found the email address
- Website
- Business phone number
- LinkedIn profile link
- Facebook business page link
- Instagram business profile link
- Date of outreach
- Method of outreach
- Multiple locations or offices
- Notes

I also developed a color-code system. Yellow was a closed sale and current client. Purple was a target client who has been reached out to. Red is do not contact ever again. (You remember the red ones, lol.) Now I could look at all outreach in a particular city like Los Angeles, California, as an example and quickly see who, when, and how I had reached out to a business.

I would research and add at least ten new businesses to the database every day, and I would prospect them as I added them either via email, LinkedIn, Facebook, or Instagram.

That was the start of the 10 + 10 Sales System!

Building the database, although manual work and somewhat tedious, was a crucial part of the sales system. As I would research every Optometry practice (my target client) in a specific city, I would always find new potential clients who had just opened, as well as ones I had never reached out to before. **Just the act of looking for all their information gave me great insight into their businesses.** I could tell a lot by their business websites and even more by looking at their social media channels.

For example, I would look at their websites and I could estimate how old they were and who they were currently using as website providers. I could do audits on their websites and SEO, which allowed me to see where they were ranking on Google and against their competitors. I would search and view their LinkedIn profiles, which would immediately tell me how active or inactive they were on that channel and if it would be worth connecting with them there. I would find their business Facebook pages and follow them, but also preview activity and what they were posting, and the same with Instagram. Now obviously this is very important research for me, as I am going to try to sell them marketing and social media management, but think of what you could find out:

- You might be able to see if they are talking about your products or competitors' products on their websites and social media

- It may give you some ideas on how you can be of assistance

- If you follow their social media posts, you will gain a clearer understanding of what's important to them (as in, products, customers, services, promotions, and so on)

The data was invaluable. It would allow me to tailor my outreach more effectively, with better results, as I was hopefully giving them a resource that was more directed at their businesses. I started to craft scripts and messaging that were specific to a connection on LinkedIn or Instagram. I began doing A/B testing, which is testing different messages to see what would work best in getting a prospect to either respond or connect back. And then I quickly realized I needed to get better organized so I could follow the same outreach system every day.

That is how I developed the **10 + 10 Sales System**.

Every day, I would do the following:

1. **Database** 10 + 10: Research and add 10 new businesses to the database and prospect 10 while adding.

2. **Email** 10 + 10: Add 10 new emails to the database and email 10 prospects.

3. **LinkedIn** 10 + 10: Find and invite 10 new prospects to connect and direct message or InMail 10 connections and share a post.

4. **Facebook** 10 + 10: Find and follow 10 prospects' business pages and comment or like 10 prospects' posts and share a post.

5. **Instagram** 10 + 10: Find and follow 10 prospects' profile pages and comment, like 10 posts, or direct message profiles that follow you back, and share a post.

That's **100** touchpoints and outreach every single day. Try doing that on a traditional sales day on the road. It's not going to happen. I could now connect and prospect a serious amount of new potential clients in just a few hours. Welcome to the world of digital and social selling.

With all your competitors trying to get their brands and products in front of clients, it's up to you to stand out and be different.

Digital outreach is way easier than cold calling!

Salespeople ask me if I still cold call at all. And my answer is, rarely. Not because I have a fear of picking up the phone, but because it just doesn't work as well as digital outreach. With cold calling, I almost always deal with a gatekeeper who has been trained to get rid of me. There is a time and place that I still use the phone, but we are talking a few times a month.

Instead of cold calling, the marketer in me knows to rephrase my approach as "warm calling." Warm, to me, is I have an in of some kind of warm opening that I can use with the gatekeeper. We belong to a few buying groups for eye care professionals, and they give us the list of all of their members. Lists are what I call warm leads. The lists only contain the business name, main contact or owner, address, and phone number, so I add them to my master database and proceed to look up as much digital information as I can about the business and owner. However, the following is one of the times I might also try calling.

 Warm call example:

Receptionist Sally answers the call:

Hi Sally. This is Trudi from Marketing4ECPs. We are a vendor with (insert group name) and I obtained your business name from their member list. I am hoping to get a chance to talk to Dr. Smith, the owner, about the digital marketing services we have to offer and some free marketing resources we have for group members.

Get over your fear of reaching out, especially if you use my methodology around giving!

I am going to teach you to **give** during outreach, so it doesn't feel like outreach. We are going to create tools and messaging that make someone want to connect with you. We are not going to send spam sales messages that immediately turn off the prospect. We are going to help you reach out the right way on the right channels to the right clients.

Sound good? Let's get started.

 Hot Points to Remember:

- **You will not find what you don't go looking for**
- **Build your list of prospects—do not just rely on a company list**
- **Track all outreach**

 **CHAPTER 4 TO-DO LIST**

	If you are using CRM (Customer Relationship Management) software, or other sales leads programs, investigate what you can track and what reporting it will give you. Pull a report of your current outreach. Add as much information as possible to this database, such as email addresses, LinkedIn profiles, Facebook pages, and Instagram profile links.
	If you don't have a CRM, or if you think a spreadsheet will work better, start building a basic tracking database with Excel and create the tabs to collect the proper information and data.

CHAPTER 5

Email 10 + 10

*Email is the Jason Bourne of online:
somebody's always trying to kill it.
It can't be done!*

—ABDUL AZIZ

Have you ever bought something that was a total waste of money and you had no way to return it? Well, that's what happened to us in our first year of business. We bought a **dud** email list.

It almost sounded too good to be true, "Buy a list of 10,000 of your targeted clients and their confirmed email addresses." Well, it was too good to be true, and we paid for it repeatedly for a long time. We added it to our current email list and sent it out through our email platform provider, and BOOM! Hundreds came back as invalid, and hundreds more were marked as spam. Now our entire email list was affected, and even legit emails would often end up in spam folders. We tried to clean out the list we bought, but it took us years to truly fix it.

Email Marketing Lesson #1: Don't buy a list, **build a list**.

Marketers know that email marketing is not only very much alive and kicking, but has an incredible ROI. For every $1 spent, email marketing generates $38 in return on investment (Source: https://www.emailmonday. com/dma-national-client-email-report-2015/). So, how can sales reps or sales teams use email marketing to their advantage?

Before you get excited and just start emailing everyone, it is imperative that you understand the laws and regulations around direct email marketing.

Because there was so much bulk spam email, countries started to put laws into effect to discourage unsolicited emails. Bulk email is the act of sending an email campaign to a large group at once. Laws you need to be aware of include, in the U.S., the CAN-SPAM Act (https://www.ftc.gov/ tips-advice/business-center/guidance/can-spam-act-compliance-guide-business). Canada has CASL (https://crtc.gc.ca/eng/internet/anti.htm) laws, and the U.K. has GDPR (https://gdpr-info.eu/). It is important for you to read and understand the laws for your particular country. For this book, we are going to concentrate on U.S. laws. However, my advice is always: know before you go or, in this case, before you send. Not following regulations can result in hefty fines.

Chances are, if you work for a large organization it is already following the email marketing laws and collecting email addresses properly. If it gives you a client list with email addresses, ensure you understand how the email was collected and any restrictions around using the email. One tip to note about a company list: **don't just rely on their list**. Company lists can be outdated and missing valuable target clients. Add or build your own list as well.

Here are a few rules of thumb to follow when considering emailing a target client. The laws stipulate that people need to give you permission to email them. Every country has a different definition of permission, but generally the two kinds are "implied permission" and "express permission":

- **Implied permission** means those people your company or you have an existing business relationship with. They could be current clients or customers or have accounts with your company.

- **Express permission** is when people give you permission to email them. For example, they have subscribed to something on your website, email, or blog platform, or downloaded something from your website. As a sales representative, this could be a verbal permission to allow communications to a client.

Before I was a marketer, I was a vision care sales rep, and I built my email database by asking every single client if I could have their direct email address and send them communications when something new came out. Because I didn't just spam them with ongoing emails, they appreciated the ones that I did send out. I also had a disclaimer at the bottom of my email that if they no longer wanted to receive emails from me, they could reply "STOP." I never had anyone ask me to STOP.

 Email Lesson Number #2: **The easiest way to get permission is to ask.**

Now that we have some of the legal stuff out of the way, let us talk about building the list.

You might have heard the saying, "The money's in the list." Like a lot of start-up businesses, we had no list. We had my network and connections, but we needed to start building our database. We built a decent-sized list that totaled about 7,000 over the years, through various events, but it wasn't until the pandemic hit in 2020 that we actually put list-building strategies into place and saw what you can do when you are focused on getting subscribers. In one year, we went from 7,000 subscribers to 29,000 subscribers—over four times' growth in sign-ups. So how did we do it?

Out of a desire to help our industry as businesses were shutting down during the initial pandemic lockdown came the realization of how to grow our database fast. Within days of the lockdown, we came out with an e-book for Optometry practices with helpful tips on communication strategies to keep in touch with patients while their practices were closed. It was not only downloaded hundreds of times, but other suppliers also asked to give it to their entire client list, which equaled FREE exposure for us. Epiphany! **Give away something your target clients need at that given moment, and you will win email subscribers.** And a little goodwill at the same time.

Next, we launched a webinar within the first week of the pandemic shutdown and instead of talking about anything marketing we brought in some of our Optometry clients to discuss how they were coping with the shutting of their businesses. We did not even mention anything about our marketing services. It was viewed thousands of times. We hosted it, so we gained a ton of exposure from being the facilitator of the webinar, and we also collected all of those email registrations. **Nothing will gain you relationships and respect as much as goodwill in times of need.** This is still paying back tenfold. Every week, someone mentions that they watched and enjoyed the webinars we did in the spring of 2020 and 2021.

Other list-building strategies we used were weekly blogs, pop-up ads on the website, a full webinar series, a web page dedicated to e-books, and a bunch of downloadable resources. We also posted blogs and resources to our social media channels to drive additional awareness and engagement and, of course, more subscribers.

As the main salesperson for our company, I also employed some personal strategies. I would research and add my target businesses to the master database and at the same time I would search for email addresses, even if just for the business. I would then cold call some of the recent additions and ask the receptionist if I could talk to the practice owner. When they (almost always) said no, I was ready by letting them know I had some amazing free marketing resources I wanted to share and some information about our services. I asked if I could email it to them. **At least 70% of the time**, the receptionist would give me the email address and permission to email them. I would track that in my database, in case the laws ever came back to bite me, along with the receptionist's name. Where can you find the email address for the business? Business websites usually have the email address, but I also check their business Facebook page (follow and add it to the database at the same time).

Next, I quickly look up the practice owners on the website and check to see if they are active on LinkedIn so I can request to connect. LinkedIn strategies are in the next chapter, but if they connect back—Boom!—you have their contact info and permission to email, as they accepted your connection. The last strategy is that we have been experimenting with a new technology called **Seamless AI**. It is a tool to look up business owners, email addresses, direct phone numbers, and more. It is connected to Sales Navigator in LinkedIn, so it aids in building a powerful list with a ton of data you can use in different lead generation strategies, email list building and marketing being one of them. This is where I would start the 10 + 10 Sales System. Research and find 10 businesses to add to the database, find as much information as possible including email, owner or decision maker, and social channels and then email 10 businesses and track in the spreadsheet.

Email Lesson Number #3: **Build the list ... hit the list ... track the hits.**

Building great email communications: I am always amazed at the blatant sales messages I get every day on email and social media.

Here's one of my favorites:

Dear Trudi, thank you for connecting. I help businesses grow with automated sales messages. Are you available for a demo on Tuesday?

Seriously, don't do this. It is not my favorite.

It has made me even more determined to NEVER send out a communication **with no value and no personalization**. Automated messages sound automated. My give-before-I-ask philosophy has worked well for me. I have gained a ton of trust and respect from the industry. Now, when I post or reach out, I have a relationship. It is much easier to ask for some business when you have built rapport there.

If you are going to reach out via email, craft a great email. Don't just wing it. Develop a bunch of scripts and test them out. Always give value away in the content of the message, whether it is a resource or a tip or a statistic—something that is relevant and current to the environment at the time.

Give value, be relevant, or be deleted.

Start with great subject lines. Think about what would make you open an email and read the contents. It is always something intriguing or even intimidating. Think of hot buttons for your target audience. What are their pain points or challenges? Start with a subject line about those. Do not add too many "marketing" or "salesy" words to the headline, as it may get flagged as spam.

 **Good Examples of Subject Lines:**

- Grow Your Business with These Top Secrets
- Don't Miss This Limited Time Special
- 3 Things You Are Doing Wrong on Social Media
- Are You Ready to Add 50 New Patients to Your Schedule?

Now for the body of the content. I recommend short, snappy emails. Maybe it's because I like shorter emails and less content, but I also find they work for me. I try to keep it to two or three paragraphs at the most, with a giveaway and a call to action.

Prepare the outreach—the give, give, give, ask concept. **Personalize the message**, give value, be helpful, be thoughtful, and be a resource. Don't just sell.

Here are a few of my top scripts that I use every day:

Cold email:

Headline: Creating a Powerful Plan for Practice Growth.

Hi Dr. Smith,

Thank you for downloading our 2022 marketing resources. We know they will be very useful in planning your digital marketing efforts. In case you missed it, there is also an on-demand webinar on the exact steps to creating a powerful marketing strategy and plan. You can access the free recording here: (insert link).

Did you know that we also offer a FREE marketing assessment and audit? We will look at your current website, social media, and Google ranking to give you a full report on what you are doing well and where you can improve. Interested? Send us your website info here: (insert link).

Last, we offer a FREE 30-minute marketing consultation. Not only will we go over the audit in detail, but we will discuss what businesses just like yours are doing to crush it every day with their digital online presence. You will feel empowered with information on how to compete every day in the online world. Book a meeting here: (insert link).

 Warm email:

Headline: FREE Resources Included in Your Membership.

Hi Dr. Smith,

Hope the weather is warm in the Bay Area and that business is good. I am reaching out as we are a supplier-vendor with your Optometry buying group (insert name). Every day, we help practices all over the U.S. grow and scale their business.

As a member of (insert name), you can access the following FREE resources:

1. *2022 Marketing Plan, Webinar, and Calendar*
2. *Top 10 Biggest Mistakes Optometrists Make with Their Marketing e-Book*
3. *On-Demand Webinars on Everything Marketing and Social Media*
4. *A 1-Hour FREE Social Media Strategy Session with Our Social Marketing Team*

We also offer a FREE website, marketing, and social media audit for every practice. We will share some impactful information on where you can improve. Book a meeting with me today.

 Hot email:

Headline: You Are Missing Out on the Top Secret to Growing Your Practice

Hi Dr. Smith,

It's been a few weeks since we chatted. I am hoping you found some of the FREE resources and links I sent helpful. If you have not had a chance to look over them, just follow this email thread to find them or reach out and I can resend.

After looking at your website audit, it is clear you have some great opportunities to get more patients who are looking for an eye care provider in your territory by showing up for more searches on Google. Here is a great blog on what makes you show up first: (insert link).

If you prefer to listen to a webinar, we have one on demand also on showing up for searches on Google: (insert link).

I would love to show you a case study on how we grow practice revenue 20% YOY with the power of Google advertising. We are a Google Premier partner, which means we work closely with Google to ensure we are creating the best ads and optimizing for the top search results. Optometrist clients who invest in Google advertising often see a minimum of 20 to 50 new patients every month. Ready to learn more? Book a meeting with me.

Track what's working to get emails opened and their responses.

 We use an email platform called Active Demand that allows us to see everything from delivery times, bounce rates, and unsubscribes to open rates. We can even schedule it to resend if the target has not opened the email. The data helps us realize if one headline works better over another or if the content is converting by resulting in clicks or downloads to the free resources we offer.

There are lots of email technologies available, such as Constant Contact, MailChimp, Mad Mimi, and Get Response, among others. But if you are a sales representative without access, you can of course send out individual emails. I send personal emails all the time. I do not always want to have to send to my entire database, and these **short, personalized emails directly from my account** often get me the best results.

If you are sending from your personal email, add a professional email signature if you don't already have one. Also add a way for people to unsubscribe, even from your personal email.

Hot Points to Remember:

- **Don't rely on a company list; build your own list**
- **Ask everyone for their email address and permission to email them**
- **Craft great outreach communications with value**

CHAPTER 5 TO-DO LIST

If your company has an account or client list you can build from, obtain that and start there. Start creating your master database, adding in additional target clients, their email address, and other social information you can find.

Come up with three attention-grabbing headlines. Experiment with ones that are more of a question and ones that intrigue the subscribers, making them want to open the email and read more.

Craft three simple outreach messages. Ensure you give value. Try the give, give, give, and ask (or call to action). It works so well, and I reuse these messages on other digital sites like LinkedIn and Instagram.

Create a professional signature if you don't have one and a one-sentence disclosure on how people can ask you to stop emailing them if they prefer.

CHAPTER 6

LinkedIn 10 + 10

92% of B2B buyers are willing to
engage with a sales professional who
has established themselves as an
industry thought leader.

—LINKEDIN: HTTPS://WWW.SLIDESHARE.NET/LINKEDIN-SALES-SOLUTIONS/
ESTABLISH-YOUR-PROFESSIONAL-BRAND

I do a lot of public speaking on marketing and sales. When I start a presentation, I like to have fun with my audience and also set the stage for being open to learning new things. Seasoned salespeople, especially, often have that look when I start training that says, "I've heard it all."

So, I start with a game—I tell them to draw a flower. No other direction except, draw a flower.

Ninety-five percent of the audience will draw the same flower: a daisy.

Why did most of them draw a daisy?

- It is the flower they know

- They have drawn it before

- It's easy

- It's what they remember

- It is the first thing that came to mind

- Somewhere, someone taught them to draw a daisy

- It is quick with little detail

This is the same thing we do in business every day:

- We do what we have always done

- We do what we know

- Someone taught us how to sell and that is what we still do

- We do what's easy

Well, I am here to tell you selling has changed. We can't do what we have always done or what worked in previous years. The buyers have changed, too. They are busy, harder to reach than they ever have been, and cautious because their landscape was pulled out from underneath them in 2020. Oh, and one more thing about the buyers: **they are online more than ever**.

Social selling and digital networking are your new cold calling. We have gone from the information economy to the knowledge and service economy to, now, the digital economy. Digital and social intelligence and how to use it to open digital doors will be the sales skill set all businesses should be teaching. In my experience, the most important social platform to learn for sales is LinkedIn. I get amazing lead generation and actual appointments with LinkedIn. It is the best digital sales tool that you have immediate, FREE access to.

But wait—before I get into how I use it, let me say this: PLEASE do not assist all the lazy, automated sales reps who send spammy sales messages three seconds after connecting by doing the same thing. What once was a professional directory and networking Mecca has turned into a breeding ground for lead generation agencies that use it to send automated connection and meeting requests and are turning people off from connecting.

That all being said, LinkedIn is still my go-to for digital prospecting. Not only are the majority of my target clients there (on LinkedIn), but many are still open to connecting and networking with salespeople. **For every ten connection requests I send out a day, I generally get three or four who connect back.** Those are pretty good odds, especially as this is the owner and decision maker who is connecting and who is usually hard to reach with traditional methods.

I have been using LinkedIn to network for over ten years. But it has been in the past five years that I have really dug in and experimented with what it can do for sales leads. Just like my dad sifted through riverbeds for gold, I sift through LinkedIn for gold (connections, that is). Let me just say up front that I will not be able to cover everything LinkedIn can do in a book chapter. Most people only use a fraction of what LinkedIn can do. Just like I did, you should take some courses on how to use all the features and options the platform has to offer. I will post a few links at the end in the homework section. I am going to concentrate my tips on what I have done with LinkedIn to generate leads and build my industry authority online.

Here is how to get started digital prospecting on LinkedIn.

Profile

It all starts with building a great profile. This is where I see salespeople leave opportunities on the table. If you ask a target client to connect with you, they will first visit your profile to find out more and make the decision to accept the request. This is your sales page and your story. Tell a great story about your current role and expertise.

Feel free to visit my LinkedIn profile and copy any of the content and strategies to build your own profile: https://www.linkedin.com/in/trudicharest/.

Add a professional image of yourself:

- Add a cover image (you can create one in Canva or search Google for LinkedIn cover images and choose a stock background). Just do not leave it the blank generic LinkedIn default generated cover.

- Add a great title. It doesn't have to be just your current role; it can also include keywords of what you do. Example: Account Manager/Business Strategist/Optical Industry Guru (except with your industry). :)

- Fill in all your contact information so a connection can easily contact you.

Now work on the next sections:

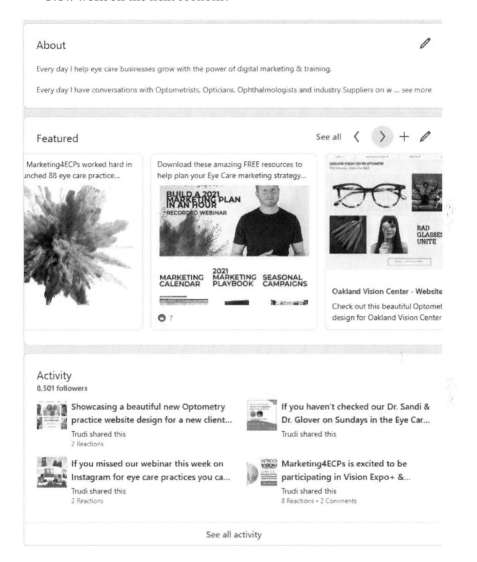

- Fill in the "About" section. This is where you can tell your story of what you do and how you help businesses in your industry. It is also a great place to put links to resources or contact information.

- Featured section is the area where you can feature images and videos of your products or services. Use great pictures and images to draw attention and link to where visitors can get additional information.

- Activity section is where you can quickly see all your current activity, like posts, shares, and comments.

Experience   +

Co-Founder I Marketer I Speaker I Consultant   ✎

Marketing4ECPs

Jul 2015 – Present · 5 yrs 11 mos

Marketing4ECPs is a full service digital marketing agency focused in the eye care industry. We're not your typical marketing agency. We won't sell you a set and forget it website. We'll recommend what works best for your business in a customized solution not a cookie cutter program. We know what turns the dial and gets results. We're working with the best partners like Google & Facebook to get you leading edge technology and expertise to help us win the competitive game of marketing.

We do it all - websites, SEO, SMS, SES, digital advertising, social media, social advertisir ...see more

Website Design

President I Founder

Jobs4ECPs

Jun 2011 – Present · 10 yrs

Jobs4ECPs is a online jobsite and community dedicated to eye care professionals. We post jobs for all eyecare sectors including Optometry, Opticianry, Ophthalmology and more. This is the best place to start your eye care job search or post a position for your next eye care employee. Visit our website today! www.Jobs4ECPs.ca (CA).

Eye Care Jobs

- Next, fill in your experience section. Think of it as more than just a resume but also a chance to sell your expertise. You can also attach an image with a link in each experience section. Do not forget to connect it to your current company.

Last, fill in the remaining sections:

Education

University of Calgary
HR Management, Human Resouces & Training
2000 – 2005

NAIT (Northern Alberta Institute of Technology)
Optician, Optics & Dispensing
1991 – 1992

Skills & endorsements

Add a new skill

Take skill quiz

Training · 99+

Endorsed by Patricia Bassendowske and 1 other who is highly skilled at this

Endorsed by 10 of Trudi's colleagues at Eye Recommend

Sales · 99+

Endorsed by Fernando Silva and 11 others who are highly skilled at this

Endorsed by 2 of Trudi's colleagues at Eye Recommend

Employee Training · 99+

Endorsed by Angela Lehmkuhle, who is highly skilled at this

Endorsed by 5 of Trudi's colleagues at Eye Recommend

Show more ⌄

Recommendations

Ask for a recommendation

Received (3)   Given (5)

Ken Barbet
President & CEO at Vision Alliance Partnership
May 9, 2012, Ken was a client of Trudi's

Find

Trudi is absolutely the hardest working person I know and her desire to produce superb and meaningful materials makes her irreplaceable.

Patricia Bassendowske
Director of Business Coaching
November 28, 2011, Trudi worked with Patricia in the same group

Find

Trudi is an inspiring speaker and creator. I worked alongside Trudi during her time as a corporate trainer at Shoppers Optical. She had the ability to identify training needs and develop course material that was spot on the mark. Trudi's presentation skills and ability to captivate her audience has an amazing impa... See more

Show more ⌄

Accomplishments

40 Publications
Viewing Sales From A Different Lens - A Prescriptive Based Approach To Sales · Your New Normal: Finding Positive Ways to Utilize Your Time in the Era of COVID-19 · Create Exceptional Kids Eyewear Experiences This Fall · 3 Biggest Marketing Mistakes Optometrists Make · Managing & Motivating Millennial Employees · Getting Your Eye Care Practice Ready for 2019 · Welcome New Employees · Blowing Out Old Product · Managing by Personality · Tips For The Eye Care Job Seeker · Put Me In Coach! · Query For Past Behaviors · 5 Ways To Grow Your Eyecare Business! · Let Them Down Easy · Turning A Negative Review Into A Positive · Service Recovery · How To Fire Staff · Stay Interviews · Performance Evaluations · Resolving Internal Conflict in your Eyecare Team...

1 Project
JOBS4ECP's "New" Eyecare Community

- Education: Straightforward. Fill out as thoroughly as possible.

- Endorsements: I found if I endorsed people, they would endorse me back.

- Recommendations: Same concept; I would ask someone to recommend me, and I would do the same in return.

- Accomplishments: I was lucky that I was an author for several industry publications over the years, so I uploaded and linked to many of my previous articles.

Now you have a robust profile page, and you are ready to get prospecting. **Start Prospecting with These Steps:**

1. Building Your Expertise:

Before you start asking every one of your target clients to connect with you, build up some activity and expert content so the prospective client you are asking to connect with can look at your profile and get an idea of what you will be sharing.

I post content five times a week, on average. I mix it up from showcasing new client website designs to sharing free resources, articles, and webinar registrations. An easy way to get started is to share posts that your current company is already posting. Or you can link to a company blog, articles, or on-demand video. Any content your company is already producing is easy content to share.

I always post with an objective in mind. I either want to educate on a specific topic, intrigue with a new website design, or catch attention with a quote or statistic that makes them think about my services without me having to "sell" them. Then I try to get them to do something with a call to action, such as "Click here" or "Book now."

Here is an example of a post I would share:

Trudi Charest
Co-Founder at 4ECPs I Business Development I Marketer I Growth Strateg...
3d •

If you missed our webinar this week on Instagram for eye care practices you can catch the recording here: https://lnkd.in/dhCPEMr We also gave away a file of summer social posts. You can download them for FREE here: https://lnkd.in/gRNE-Cr #optometry #optical #optometrist #digitalmarketing #socialmedia #instagram

 2

👍 Like   💬 Comment   ↪ Share   ✈ Send

 152 views of your post in the feed

I also watch the analytics. I want to see likes and comments (because then it shows in their connection feed as well), and I watch how many views it generated. It gives me a good idea of which content is performing well, and I try to post more of that for future content.

2. Inviting People to Connect:

I actively search and send connection invitations to at least ten target clients every day. I then send out ten direct messages to connections and track them in the master database I created to monitor and track all outreach. This is part of the 10 + 10 Sales System, and it works very well. I see on average three to four connect back with me out of the ten requests per day, and I have ten years of connections to reach out to (almost 9K at the time of this book release), so I am messaging target clients every day on LinkedIn. Some salespeople might get disappointed in the results because I can connect and message one hundred people before I might get a response or a booked demo, but I tell myself it's "**planting seeds**." I know that my outreach is not always going to generate an immediate response and that's OK; it is a long-term strategy. But I will say this: I see it working every day. I have had a demo with a potential client who appears to have come through by way of a Facebook ad to only tell me in person that they see me on LinkedIn every week. I have also seen a potential client reach back out to me a year after I originally messaged them. Plant seeds. Every day!

Activity breeds activity.

OK, let's get searching for target clients. You can start with generic searches like the title of the target client and, in this case, I also want only the business owners. My target client is an optometrist practice owner, so I start there. I can also add territory, such as the city and state they practice in.

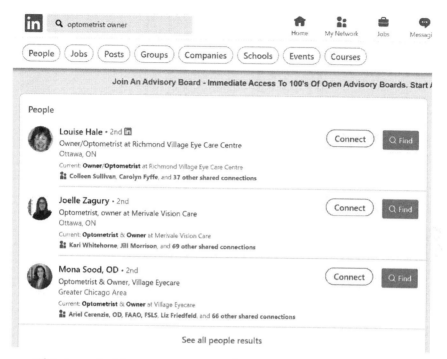

This is probably a great time to chat about the standard LinkedIn account versus a premium account. I used a standard or basic account for literally the first six years I had a LinkedIn account, so do not feel you need to immediately jump to a premium account. Although premium does have its benefits, like advanced searches, additional invitations, direct InMails, and premium-to-premium free messaging. I make use of all of them every month. My recommendation would be to start with a standard account, and start connecting and networking and building your expertise. When you are feeling like you are starting to understand the platform, you can take better advantage of the FREE thirty-day trial of premium because there are also a few different premium accounts to test. About five years ago, I upgraded to premium and did the basic business premium. Last year, I changed and upgraded again to the Sales Navigator Premium, which is a must if you are doing the amount of prospecting I am now doing on LinkedIn. It helps me track all my outreach and build different target lists. This keeps me better organized.

Once I search and find a target client, I want to first preview their profile. I am looking for a few things. The number one thing I am looking for is if they are active on LinkedIn. You only get to send so many connections a day. It used to be a hundred a day, but with new changes to the platform, it is now one hundred per week. I do not want to "waste" a connection request on someone who created a profile and never visits the platform. How do I tell? I look at how many connections they have and their activity feed. If they have less than one hundred connections, I pass. Over one hundred, I invite to connect.

Once you click the connect button, it will ask you to send or add a note. Adding a note is putting a personal message in the invitation. I always try to add a personal note. It tends to get way better results than the generic invite that says, "I would like to add you to my professional network."

Add a note to your invitation   ✕

LinkedIn members are more likely to accept invitations that include a personal note.

> Hi Louise...great to see you on OWA webinar. I would love to connect on LinkedIn. |

216 / 300

Cancel   **Send**

 A few more tips about finding target clients:

- When you have a target client profile open, you can click on their personal connections and browse through for more options. In my industry, optometrists always connect with other optometrists, so they have a wealth of "colleagues" in their network.

- On the right-hand side of a client profile is a section called "People also viewed" with more connection options usually related to that client search.

- Try additional keyword searches and direct searches by name.

- Visit profiles of your competitors and other sales reps in your industry and again look at "People also viewed" on the right-hand side.

3. Using InMail:

I love, love, love InMail. While you can direct message anyone on LinkedIn who has accepted your connection request, what if they do not connect with you or you want to reach out directly to a non-connection? Say hello to InMail. InMail lets you send a private message to anyone who is not a direct connection. With a premium account you receive fifteen to twenty InMail communications every month. Here's another great feature: if you send an InMail and the person accepts it and responds, you get that InMail credit back. I use all of my InMail credits every month and actively target "big" opportunity clients with them.

What to send in the message? Similar to sending an attention-grabbing email, you'll want to do the following:

- Write a great subject line

- Keep it short and specific

- Personalize if you can

- Make it valuable and give them something for free

- Ask them to connect only, not to set up a sales meeting

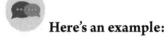

Here's an example:

Subject Line: FREE Summer Social Media Posts!

Hey Dr. Smith ... hope all is well. I am the Co-Founder of Marketing4ECPs, a digital agency for Optometrists. We are known for building the most beautiful websites in eye care (check this one out! https://parkslopeeye.com/) and the best digital advertising that gets you results and new patients.

We just did a webinar on "Instagram for Eye Care" and the recording is available on demand on our website, as well as the giveaway of 30 summer Instagram posts for immediate download here: https://marketing4ecps.com/summer-social-media-downloads/.

If there is anything we can help you out with as far as your practice marketing, please reach out. Would love to connect! Thanks, Trudi

4. Direct Messaging:

Once someone accepts your connection request, they are considered a first connection. You are now allowed to directly message them. But here is my direct message tip: don't message them right away. Wait a few days or even a week. Let them see a few of your posts during the week and get to know you a bit.

Use the same tips as above in the InMail message. Make the first direct message personal and valuable. Do not ask them for a sales meeting. You know the saying, "Pressure makes diamonds." Not here. No pressure = happy connections. Pressure = un-connections.

Example I Use Every Single Day:

Hey Dr. Smith. Thanks for connecting!

Just reaching out to share some FREE resources for 2022, including a recorded webinar on building an eye care marketing plan for your practice, a marketing calendar, a 2022 marketing playbook, and a file of seasonal social media campaigns... all for immediate download here: https://marketing4ecps. com/2022-marketing-plan/.

We are a digital marketing agency for Optometrists. If there is anything we can help you with as far as marketing, please reach out. Thank you, Trudi

Secret Tip for Direct Messages:

This one took me a long time to figure out on my own, so I am excited to share this tip with you. I found groups in my industry on LinkedIn and joined as many as I could (50, to be exact). Some had 20 to 30,000 members. I was super active in a couple of the bigger groups, posting and sharing content, when I figured out almost by accident that I could **direct message anyone in the group**, even those who are not connected to me in any way. This was huge! I could now actively reach out to my target clients without having to connect at all. Game changer! I now spend a few minutes every day direct messaging ten new targets in a group: 10 + 10.

5. Interacting:

Interaction on social channels has been my competitive advantage for staying ultra-visible and active. I like, comment, and share industry posts all the time. But here is one way to get the attention of your target connections: comment on their posts. Say something positive or congratulatory without sounding like you are sucking up. Nothing wins relationships like compliments and kudos. It also allows you to remind them of you and your business without actively trying to sell to them. Remember ... planting seeds.

Another way to interact and find more connections is to like a target client's business page on LinkedIn. They will see you are following them on their business pages and hence see your name again, but you can also see who else works there. I click on the link that says, "All employees who work here" and proceed to view the opportunities to connect. Although I often only go after the owner, it is also lucrative to look for additional business co-owners or managers of the business and try to connect with them.

I spend at least an **hour** on LinkedIn every day. It pays off in good-quality leads and connections.

Hot Points to Remember:

- **Use digital and social intelligence to open digital doors**
- **Activity breeds activity**
- **Plant seeds every day**

 **CHAPTER 6 TO-DO LIST**

	If you haven't already set up your LinkedIn account and built a great profile page, here is a link to a tutorial: https://business.linkedin.com/en-uk/marketing-solutions/blog/posts/content-marketing/2017/17-steps-to-a-better-LinkedIn-profile-in-2017.
	Follow your company business page and like or share company posts. Aim to post a minimum of 3x a week.
	Start connecting. Start by inviting people you know and those who will accept your request to build up your volume of connections. Colleagues and industry friends work great to build a base of connections. Now start searching for your target client and send out ten connection requests each day.
	Build a direct message template you can use and personalize for outreach.
	Find industry groups to join by searching industry keywords. Message ten target clients in the group with a direct message. See https://www.linkedin.com/help/linkedin/answer/186/find-and-join-a-linkedin-group?lang=en.
	More questions and answers about LinkedIn: https://www.linkedin.com/help/linkedin.
	Great blog post on LinkedIn tools for salespeople: https://nealschaffer.com/linkedin-tools/.

CHAPTER 7

Instagram 10 + 10

*Think of social selling like dating.
Once you find a prospect to connect with,
build a relationship first, before you propose.*

—TRUDI CHAREST

In case you haven't figured it out yet, I'm an overachiever. Five kids in my family, and I am the second-youngest. I grew up competing for attention, food, space, rights, and privacy. I have such great memories of growing up. Our house was always busy. When it wasn't full of our friends, it was full of our huge extended family network of aunts, uncles, and cousins.

We grew up playing games: card games, board games, outdoor games, and sports like soccer and baseball. I learned competitiveness at an early age and can honestly say I thrive on it. Just say the word "win" and I'm in.

That's why sales is a perfect occupation for me. I love the win.

I think all the competition growing up also gave me FOMO! I have always had a fear of missing out. I needed to be involved in everything. I also needed to be an expert at everything. That same drive has stayed with me through university, my career, and now running a business. I had a personal motto that if I was going to do anything, I was going to do it well and be the best at it. I will probably be 80 and kicking all the seniors' asses on the lawn bowling field. I can't help myself. :)

Well, that's the same reason I have to check out every new social media option and master it, not just dabble and post a few posts but like literally learn it from the basics up and learn exactly how I can use it for marketing, exposure, and, of course, sales.

We started the Marketing4ECPs Instagram business page in 2015 with slow but steady success. As we were still a start-up, we didn't have an internal marketing team, so we all just took turns posting and there was no plan or strategy or even consistency for the first few years. We started to truly grow our brand and followers by building beautiful posts with lots of valuable content, including contests, giveaways, downloads, and useful resources.

It was about this time that Facebook had purchased Instagram and both channels started to change the algorithms for business pages. They were both becoming a pay-to-play model. If you weren't boosting or sponsoring posts, only a small percentage of your followers would see your content. **But what had not changed were personal Instagram accounts.** I quickly started up a personal Instagram account and, knowing I was only going to use it for posting business-related content, I also set it up with a business handle, @eyecaremarketer. If you decide to set up an account you will use only for business, you can either use your name (but then don't post personal) or you can come up with something fun related to your industry or service. I chose @eyecaremarketer and it's worked well because it shows up if anyone is searching for eye care marketing and also for the term "eyecare."

I knew that to stand out and get followers in my industry I needed to do something different. I decided I was going to be known for creating fun, motivational, and inspiring quotes or sayings completely related to eye care. It was an instant hit. I had found a niche that no one else was doing and gained a huge following quickly. Just to make it even more appealing—almost every one of my followers was a potential prospect. If they weren't a prospect, they were from the industry, so it meant that I was still gaining industry exposure.

Now I had to figure out how to use it as a sales tool.

 The first sales opportunity I noticed was during the setup. The actual profile and amount of information you can post in your bio is limited, so you need to take advantage of the space available. The maximum number of characters allowed in the bio is 150. So first I changed my name, Trudi Charest, to "Digital Marketing Social Media" in the settings. You can either leave it as you, or change it to what you do or what you sell. Then I came up with five subject lines that would explain what I do without sounding too salesy. I edited the bio on my smartphone so I could add some fun industry-related emojis. And last, I found a cool digital technology that I added at the end of the bio called LinkTree. Before I explain LinkTree, know that instead of adding a technology like LinkTree, you can just add a phone number and a website link in the bio.

eyecaremarketer   Edit Profile   ○

508 posts   2,853 followers   5,719 following

Digital Marketing Social Media
Eye Care Marketer
Practice Management Speaker
Optical Influencer
Entrepreneur
Business Consultant
Free Eye Care Resources
linktr.ee/eyecaremarketer

LinkTree is a FREE technology platform that allows you to create a personalized and easily customizable page that houses all the important links you want to share with your audience. This has now assisted me in developing different links in the drop-down to drive traffic to different parts of our company website and resources.

I change the topics and content regularly and try different calls to action. The ones that still get the most traction are the FREE giveaways or downloads and webinars. I win leads as people register for something and give their contact info, and now I have them in my email database. View my LinkTree live here: https://linktr.ee/eyecaremarketer.

Eye Care Marketing Expert

Co-Founder of Marketing4ECPs. A digital marketing agency for eye care.

Download Resources: Build Your 2021 Eye Care Marketing Plan & Resources!

Let Me Do A FREE Marketing & Social Media Audit For Your Practice

Webinar: Does Social Media Earn Me New Eye Care Patients?

We Build The Most Beautiful Practice Websites In Eye Care! Check them out

Top 10 Biggest Mistakes Eye Care Businesses Are Making With Their Marketing - Ebook

EyeInnovate - The Leading Business & Growth Conference for Eye Care

OWA Podcast - Digital Networking & Social Selling

Webinar: Optometry Website Marketing For Dummies with Eyetrepreneur

E-commerce Options For Eye Care E-book. Instant Download.

Book a FREE Marketing & Website Analysis For Eye Care Practices

Join Our LI Group - Optometrist Marketing & Growth Strategies

Connect with me on LinkedIn For More Cool Ways To Grow Your Eyecare Business!

Learn More About Eye Care Marketing & Digital Marketing

Now you have your bio completed, you need a posting strategy.

I wanted to create something different and unique, as well as what would get engagement and followers. I played around with some fun quotes and sayings, and I have built what is almost a cult following with industry prospects who will "wait" every day to see what I am going to post. My posts get on average twenty-five to one hundred likes and comments every single day. (That's really good, by the way ... anything above five is a true win.)

@eyecaremarketer:

I follow lots of amazing sales reps who have figured out how to make it work for them. Check out one of my favorite industry sales gals. She crushes it on Instagram, Facebook, and LinkedIn every week. You will quickly see by her posts that she sells designer eyeglass frames to optical stores and Optometry offices.

@girlgotglasses (with permission):

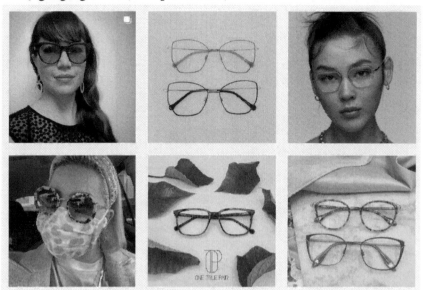

Look for content from your current company that you can repost. Take pictures with your smartphone as you are in and out of client offices and post them. Find a strategy and niche in your industry and build around that.

Some tools I use for posting:

- To create posts I use Canva, a free graphic design platform where you can easily create posts for Instagram, as well as for other social media: https://www.canva.com/

- For scheduling and planning the posts I use Later, a platform to help you organize, analyze, and schedule your posts: https://later.com/

- To repost other people's posts, I use Repost for Instagram. Download the app from the app store: https://repostapp.com/

Let's talk captions and hashtags.

Captions are important, as they have the ability to add more context and description to the image. You also can tell a deeper story about the brand or service. It also allows you to direct people to a call to action. It tells people where to buy, where to find more information, or about promotional activity.

Hashtags are essentially the search or sorting process on Instagram. Instagram aggregates all posts into # categories, which allows users to find specific content faster. Using industry, product, or service-related hashtags will assist your target client in finding you and your feed. I built a database of every hashtag I could come up with or find in my direct industry. I put it into an easy-to-access word file that I pull from every day. That way I don't have to come up with new hashtags or reuse the same hashtags over and over.

Want my list of hashtags and keywords? Go to my website under resources and download: www.thedigitalsalesrep.com. (Sorry, they are for the most part eye care-related.)

Get your target audience to follow you.

Now that you have built an account and have some posts up, how do you get followers? I have had great success by following those whom I want to follow me back. They often do! Just type into the search field who you are looking for:

- Follow your colleagues

- Follow your target clients

- Follow your target clients' businesses

- Follow your company

- Follow those who are following your company

- If you're competitive like me, follow those who are following your competitors

Now, here's where the gold is when it comes to getting more followers and leads:

- Like the posts of your target clients

- Comment on the posts of your target clients

- Like or react to their stories

Last, my secret sales weapon on Instagram is … **direct messaging**. Once a target client has started following me, I do a few things:

- I check to see if I am following them and, if not, I follow them back as well

- I immediately like or comment on their latest post

- I wait three to five days and then I send them a direct message

Hey Family Eyecare...thanks for following and liking my posts. I am the Co-Founder of Marketing4ECPs, a digital agency for Optometrists. We just did a webinar on "Instagram for Eye Care" and the recording is available on demand on our website as well as the giveaway of 30 summer Instagram posts for immediate download here: https://marketing4ecps.com/summer-social-media-downloads/. If there is anything we can help you out with as far as your practice marketing please reach out. Thanks, Trudi

Summer Social Media Downloads
Are you ready to increase your sales for sunglasses this summer? Check out our free social media downloads that include a variety of posts that you can use to promote your business throughout this season!

My first direct message is always thanking them for following and offering some type of free resource. I never try to sell them anything. My goal is to engage first, then build a relationship and keep them aware of our company.

10 + 10 on Instagram

Every single day, I follow ten accounts—either personal or business—comment on and like posts in my feed, and direct message ten accounts: 10 + 10. On average, I get a reaction or response from at least one of those to whom I sent a direct message. My odds on Instagram have been pretty good. For every hundred direct messages, I get one that gives me a meeting. And it is usually a new client with whom I would not have connected any other way. I close at least one client a month because of my efforts on Instagram. It works. Although that might sound like enough for you, all efforts compound. What I do on LinkedIn, Instagram, Facebook, and email helps everywhere else. Keep planting seeds ... they bloom in other places.

It took me a few years to grow my following to 3,000, so don't panic if it takes a while. Better to have the right followers than a ton of followers. As with other social channels, I remind myself that I am gaining exposure and planting seeds. I am always thinking about long-term exposure and awareness. If they're interested in my company or services, they will let me know.

I also started an Instagram account for salespeople, with tips and quotes to inspire you every day in digital sales. Join here: https://www.instagram.com/digitalsalesrep/.

 Hot Points to Remember:

- **Think of Instagram and sales like dating**

- **Follow to get followers**

- **Give something to receive something**

✓ CHAPTER 7 TO-DO LIST

	If you don't have an Instagram account, set one up now. Instructions here: https://help.instagram.com/155940534568753.
	Follow sales reps in your industry, especially competitors, to see what they are posting.
	Find out more about LinkTree here: https://linktr.ee/.
	Follow all your colleagues, target clients, and target businesses, as well as your own company.
	Build simple, short message scripts to use in direct messaging efforts.
	Join Digital Sales Rep on Instagram: https://www.instagram.com/digitalsalesrep/.

CHAPTER 8

Facebook 10 + 10

*The modern consumer is digitally
driven, socially connected, and
mobile empowered. Sales reps need
to adapt or be replaced.*

—JILL ROWLEY

In 1961 Vince Lombardi, coach of the Green Bay Packers, walked into the first day of training camp. The Packers had been on a bit of a losing streak in previous seasons, and they were eager to get coaching and training that would help them win games. Coach Lombardi told the team they were going back to the basics, and he literally had them start training on everything from how to hold a football properly to running lengths and sprinting drills—definitely back to basics. The players were frustrated with the basic training and mocked the coach behind his back.

Six months later, the Green Bay Packers beat the New York Giants 37–0 to win the NFL Championship. When asked by the media what the catalyst was for the change in the team, the players all said it was the excellent training and coaching they received from Coach Lombardi. **What they once complained about, they were now giving full credit for their success.**

Most salespeople don't have a coach to rely on. Some have never even had basic sales skills training, let alone been taught how to use digital channels to sell. So, you need to be your own coach.

Coach yourself like you are an NFL football player:

- Set high expectations

- Study the competition

- Watch your own plays so you can see where you can improve

- Have a goal and a vision of how to get there

- Stay fit, eat well, work out, get lots of sleep

- Kick your own ass

- Prepare for the day

- Review losses

- Celebrate wins

- Go harder next time.

Train yourself like you are an NFL football player:

- Go back to the basics (greeting, opening, closing, overcoming objections)

- Run drills; do the same thing over and over again until you get it right (10+10)

- Do more than your competition is willing to do

- Work hard ... really hard

Either you run the day,
or the day runs you.

—JIM ROHN

Training Yourself to Sell Digitally

As part of my digital sales training, I knew that Facebook had to be a great place to connect, network, and build relationships with my potential clients, but I had to train myself not only on the basics of Facebook but also on how I was going to use it as a lead-generating machine.

Facebook is the largest social network, with over 2.74 billion users at the time of writing this book (Source: https://blog.hootsuite.com/facebook-statistics/). Clearly, many of my target clients were on the platform, either for personal use or business purposes. But how should I use it for sales?

I only signed up for a Facebook profile so I could use it for business over ten years ago. I quickly realized that you must tread carefully if using it for prospecting. It's an engagement platform and it's easy to come across as salesy unless you use it in the right way. Let's face it, most people are on Facebook for personal social time. They do not want to be bombarded with direct messages about products or services.

Salespeople need to learn how to navigate the engagement and relationship factors and not spam followers and friends with ongoing sales posts. You might be asking why Instagram is different from Facebook. Well, it is a social networking channel, to be sure, but it has also been widely used by businesses to visually display their products and services, so users seem to be more tolerant of direct outreach on Instagram. I also feel from my experience that not many salespeople are using Instagram as a sales tool and outreach opportunity, so it has not been bombarded with direct messaging.

How to Start Using Facebook Every Day for Sales

1. Create a great profile:

Start by uploading a great profile picture and cover image. You can find cover images by searching on Google, creating them in Canva, or using photos from your phone. Keep them generic and simple. Something new to the profile is the ability to add a sentence and a URL below your name. As you can see, I put some information about digital marketing and a link to our company website.

Trudi Charest

Need Digital Marketing? We do digital marketing & social media for eyecare! www.marketing4ecps.com

Fill in every piece of information the platform allows you to add, such as work and employer (and link to them), education, location, address, phone number, email address, websites links, other social media channels, and more. Not only will this allow others to easily contact you or find you in other channels, but it gives you the ability to do the same. Once you find a target client and connect with them, you can view their contact information. Now you may have access to their cell phone and email address.

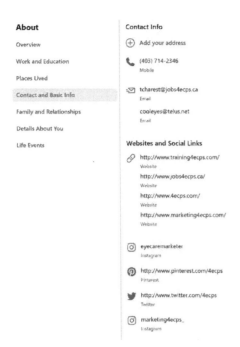

https://www.facebook.com/TrudiCharest

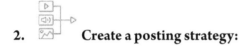

2. **Create a posting strategy:**

I do not post a ton of personal posts on Facebook. I use Facebook very differently than I do LinkedIn or Instagram. First, I don't want to spam my actual friends who are following me with a bunch of business posts, so I do a combination of a few personal posts and a few engaging business posts. And they are not sales related at all.

However, I follow some amazing salespeople who do use their personal profile to post product- or service-related posts, and they are doing a great job of managing a personal and business feed. Find a few in your industry and follow them to see what they post.

An easy way to share business posts is to follow your current company and reshare their content. You can reuse the content strategy you have for other channels like LinkedIn and Instagram.

3. 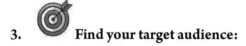 **Find your target audience:**

There are four ways you can connect with your target audience on Facebook:

- Personal connection to an individual
- Follow a target business
- Join Facebook groups that target clients may also be following
- Start your own Facebook group

Personal connecting is straightforward: type their names into the search field and once you find them click on "Add friend." If they accept and add you as a friend, you can now direct message them. You will now see their posts and videos and they will see your posts. I would start by liking and commenting on their posts. This will show your engagement. Wait a few days or even weeks before direct messaging and keep it light. Thank them for connecting.

4. **Follow a target business:**

Type the name of the business in the search field and once you find the target client business page click the "Like" button. Now you will see their posts in your daily feed. Like and comment on their posts. They will see your name over and over again, building a stronger connection and rapport.

5. **Join Facebook groups in your industry:**

Facebook groups are my secret weapon when it comes to being able to prospect by answering questions posted by my target client. For example, one group I belong to has over 40K members and the majority of them are potential clients for me. They often ask each other questions about their businesses. I watch or trawl the site daily to see if they ask any marketing or social media questions and then I quickly offer my advice or information. It has easily garnered a minimum of a few leads a week, with many asking for more information or an actual demo. To find current Facebook groups, start by typing in industry keywords, then press search. For example, I typed in "eyecare," then searched, and on the next drop-down I chose "groups" to filter all the groups with the words "eyecare" in them.

Here's an example of a question I responded to recently in an industry Facebook group:

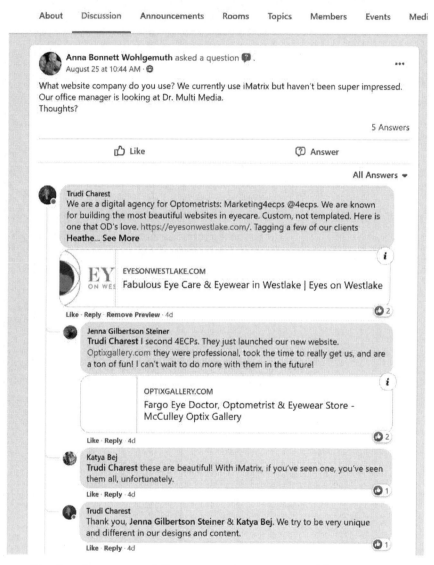

OD Divas

🔒 Private group · 7.9K members

About · Discussion · Announcements · Rooms · Topics · Members · Events · Medi

Anna Bonnett Wohlgemuth asked a question 💬 .
August 25 at 10:44 AM · 🌐

What website company do you use? We currently use iMatrix but haven't been super impressed. Our office manager is looking at Dr. Multi Media. Thoughts?

5 Answers

👍 Like   ❓ Answer

All Answers ▾

Trudi Charest
We are a digital agency for Optometrists: Marketing4ecps @4ecps. We are known for building the most beautiful websites in eyecare. Custom, not templated. Here is one that OD's love. https://eyesonwestlake.com/. Tagging a few of our clients Heathe... See More

> **EYESONWESTLAKE.COM**
> Fabulous Eye Care & Eyewear in Westlake | Eyes on Westlake

Like · Reply · Remove Preview · 4d   👍 2

Jenna Gilbertson Steiner
Trudi Charest I second 4ECPs. They just launched our new website. Optixgallery.com they were professional, took the time to really get us, and are a ton of fun! I can't wait to do more with them in the future!

> **OPTIXGALLERY.COM**
> Fargo Eye Doctor, Optometrist & Eyewear Store - McCulley Optix Gallery

Like · Reply · 4d   👍 2

Katya Bej
Trudi Charest these are beautiful! With iMatrix, if you've seen one, you've seen them all, unfortunately.

Like · Reply · 4d   👍 1

Trudi Charest
Thank you, **Jenna Gilbertson Steiner** & **Katya Bej**. We try to be very unique and different in our designs and content.

Like · Reply · 4d   👍 1

I look at how many followers are in a group and how many posts are posted on average every day or week to decide which ones are active enough for me to join. Then I request to join. If they have posts every day, it's a good group. Once in the groups, follow and monitor the posts. I also read the rules for the group. If it says do not post anything promotional, I don't. If it appears you can post, I will share a post every other week on something like an upcoming webinar or a free resource. I never post a direct solicitation for business, only a freebie of some kind. I get a few responses, but I know it gets attention and my brand is getting exposure. I follow over seventy groups, so I have a system I use to keep track of where I am able to post and where I just monitor. There are a few groups where I get most of the traction from, so I ensure I visit those groups daily.

6.   Start your own Facebook group:

One way to get away from the rules is to start your own group. I have now started three groups. I chose each group title to be something that is interesting and engaging to my target client and is easily searchable. My most popular group is "Optometry & Eyecare Marketing." It is not branded as my company, but I am the admin. I also get to control who is able to join the group, so I reject any of my marketing competitors. I send out invitations to my network to connect. Now I can post anything I want in the group and get direct access to target clients with whom I would not have connected otherwise. Win-win.

The other thing I love about Facebook groups is that there is no restriction at this time about how many of your followers will see your posts—like what is happening with business pages. A Facebook business page has become a pay-to-play model, but right now, Facebook groups are free. When you post in the group, it alerts the followers in their daily notifications that there is a new post in the group. It's almost a call to action to go to the group and look at what was recently posted. I post with my same philosophy of giving something away to get them to do another action, like downloading or signing up for something.

Here's an example:

Trudi Charest
Admin · May 21 at 11:49 AM · 🌐

If you missed our webinar this week on Instagram you can catch the recording here: https://marketing4ecps.com/our-webinars/We also gave away a file of summer social posts. You can download them for FREE here: https://marketing4ecps.com/summer-social-media-downloads/ #optometry #optical #optometrist #digitalmarketing #socialmedia #instagram

PS: I also created a Facebook group just for us: Digital Sales Reps. Join us as we share success strategies on all things sales: https://www.facebook.com/groups/1092012964613017

BONUS

7. ☰ **Bonus Strategy:**

I saw an amazing sales and marketing strategy that I recently tested out myself. It was shared by an agency coaching service that can be found at www.agencycoach.com. It worked so well, it is going to become my "go-to" prospecting strategy on Facebook and I am going to test it out on other channels as well. In Canva, I made a very simple graphic and input the text, "I have created a simple step-by-step guide to get better ranking on Google without using ads. Who wants it?" I posted it to one of the larger Optometry groups I belong to. Over 700 target clients said they wanted it, 150 gave me their direct email address, and others asked me to direct message them, which means they need to receive my message request. I had the actual step-by-step guide ready to send to them, as well as a place where they can download it by giving me their email address.

Talk about an easy way to get the attention of hundreds of potential customers! What can you create that your target audience would want so bad they will give you their email addresses to get it?

I have created a simple step by step guide on how to get better ranking on Google without using ads.
Who wants it?

Want the guide? I will give you my copy for FREE and you can use it or create your own: www.thedigitasalesrep.com.

If I haven't convinced you yet to use social selling and digital networking as a part of your daily prospecting strategy, then maybe these stats will help you see the light:

- As a part of their sales process, 73% of salespeople use social selling to outperform their sales peers

- Salespeople who mix social selling into their sales process exceeded quota 23% more often

- By using social selling techniques, 79% of salespeople achieve their quotas

(Source: https://blog.zoominfo.com/b2b-social-selling/)

Facebook has helped me land lots of clients. It's also not going away, so the sooner you jump in and test the waters, the sooner you will find out how easy it is to connect, network, and sell on Facebook.

 Hot Points to Remember:

- **Train yourself to sell digitally**

- **Like and comment on posts with easy, no-pressure tactics**

- **Facebook groups are your secret weapon**

CHAPTER 8 TO-DO LIST

	If you don't have a Facebook account, set one up now. Instructions are here: https://www.facebook.com/help/188157731232424.
	Follow sales reps in your industry, especially competitors, to see what they are posting.
	Follow all your colleagues, target clients, and target businesses, as well as your own company.
	Follow all the industry groups you can find by typing in keywords.
	Join the Digital Sales Rep Group on Facebook: https://www.facebook.com/groups/1092012964613017.

CHAPTER 9

Batter Up—Virtual Demos

*Success today requires the agility
and drive to constantly rethink,
reinvigorate, react, and reinvent.*

—BILL GATES

I'm either out or I'm all in. I never do things half-assed. If I can't do something really well, I don't do it. Period.

It was early in my career as an optician, when I was managing a large retail optical store, that I experienced actual sales skills training for the first time. The chain I was working for decided to train every employee in the organization on sales and customer service skills and then instigate a standards program. They trained on some of these basic skills:

- Greeting the customer within thirty seconds
- Using proper greetings
- Building rapport
- Asking lifestyle questions

- Overcoming objections
- Asking for the business

Then they sent mystery shoppers out every month to shop employees on sales and customer service skills and report back on the results. The first reports were dismal. It seemed like a huge failure. Undaunted, the company continued with further training and more mystery shopping. The results were slightly better but nowhere near successful. Then the president of the company came to visit my location. He asked me for feedback on why I thought the results were so poor. I said, without any hesitation: **"Because no one has committed to doing it 100% of the time."** It was even eye-opening to me as I said it because, yes, I had not been doing it 100% of the time, or even 50% of the time for that matter, and I was the leader of that location. So, if I wasn't doing it, neither were my employees.

 Commitment is the key to any success.

I realized I could not judge this program without giving it the proper dedication, so that Monday I decided to do everything exactly as it had been taught. It took a little finessing and tweaking to find my way around the different parts of the sales program, but it started to feel more natural and guess what! It started to work. Not only was I closing sales left and right, but I was also closing bigger sales than I ever had—and multiple sales. Guess what else started to happen! **My staff noticed and started doing it too.**

This was one of many business and sales lessons I would learn over the years. There are a few that will always stick with me:

- Be open to new ideas
- Help others become successful
- Do more than you are asked to do
- Show up
- Be there fully

- Be prepared

- Know your part

- Outwork your competition

- Be professional always

- Look for the lessons

Business is ever-changing.

You need to be open to change. As we all experienced in 2020, life and business can change in a minute. You need to be agile, adaptive, and innovative if you are going to compete and survive in the world of sales. Sales has become an online sport and if you are not using digital, you are missing out and losing sales.

It's like a batter going up to bat without a bat!

One thing is clear: organizations that train their sales reps on digital and social selling will win sales. Give the batter a bat.

So, what happens once you make a connection? Batter up ....

Here is what happened once I started making connections on email, LinkedIn, Instagram, and Facebook: BAM! I was landing sales demos, inquiries, and meetings. Now I had to learn how to do remote meetings. Like everyone else around the world, we all quickly learned about virtual meetings and online platforms like Zoom.

It happened so fast, the transition to digital demonstrations, that the first few "virtual demos" were a testing of the waters and I realized I needed some insights and a plan. I needed to understand what was engaging during a virtual demonstration to secure a sale. I have since perfected the virtual demo and I want to share a wealth of tips and tricks I learned along the way.

1. Learn all virtual meeting platforms:

Clients may not be as digitally adept as you are, which is why you should be ready and able to present on any platform they know and are comfortable with. I can easily do Google Hangouts, Zoom, GoToMeetings, Microsoft Teams, or Skype. Be knowledgeable in as many as you can.

2. Send meeting invite and confirm:

After a few "missed" meetings, I started sending out the digital invite from the platform, but I follow up with a direct email and link to the meeting. I also wait about five minutes into the meeting and, if the client has not arrived by then, I send another email with the same link and they almost always show up. Make it easy to find the link to the meeting.

3. Arrive early:

I always arrive early to the meeting link, ready to go as soon as the client arrives. One out of five clients arrive early, and I always look at this as additional sales minutes, which are invaluable.

4. Ask how much time they have:

I am usually dealing with busy doctors, so time is of the essence. I ask them how much time they have, and I stick to it, even if I don't get through the entire presentation. I get them back to their patients on time. This shows respect and time management.

5. Be prepared:

I do all my prep work early in the morning, so even if I get sidetracked during the day, I have all the intel and analytics ready to start my conversation with the prospect. I have examples and reports up and ready to click on my computer tabs. I also have databases open in case I need to grab a different example. Yes, every once in a while I need to pull something up while I am talking, but for the most part I am ready to go and they appreciate that.

6. Be ready to troubleshoot:

You are dealing with technology and sometimes clients are not entirely digital experts, so be ready to help with things like volume, unmuting, video, and so on. I often get clients using their computers at the office and they don't realize until we're on the demo that they don't have speakers on that computer. I quickly ask them for their cell number or work number if they have a phone near the computer so we can chat via phone but still screen share. Also, don't react, or go silent—just keep talking and work the situation out. Be ready in every situation.

7. Headset ready to go:

Invest in a good headset. Depending on your situation, you need to ensure you don't have any distracting background noise. If you do hear any weird static or echo sounds, then try to fix them before beginning your presentation. Ask the clients if they are hearing you OK. A bad connection can ruin the demo. I have also asked a client to disconnect and then come back in to see if that fixes it, and sometimes it does.

8. Background:

I spent almost a year working and selling from home. During those initial meetings, I kept seeing the background of my office and realized I needed to spruce it up a bit. I put a plant and some artwork behind me and now it looks visually attractive and appealing, but not distracting. Find a background that is not showing activity, if possible. You want the client focused on you. Some virtual platforms like Zoom let you load "fake" backgrounds.

9. First few minutes:

I spend the first few minutes of the meeting doing what I would do if it were a live meeting. I greet them, introduce myself and my company, and then I build some rapport. I have come prepared with something that I have found we either have in common or a piece of information to open the conversation. Go back to your sales skills.

10. Ask questions:

I get to know them first before diving into the sales process and presentation. I ask a ton of questions about their businesses, goals, challenges, and objectives. I also ask them how they heard of us and what brought them to us that day. It often leads to information I will bring back into the close of the conversation.

11. Show yourself on video:

I can't tell you how many people I have had meetings with who don't turn on their video. I have had some say to me, "Oh, I am super casual today and no makeup," or "I am eating lunch." Hey, I am all about multitasking, but don't let that ever be you with a potential client. Get up, get dressed, put on makeup, do your hair, look the part. Virtual or not. Your client can be casual and no video, but you can't.

12. Check your settings:

Make sure your screen resolution is the correct size for the platform you are on and looks good in a presentation. I was on a call with a technology company I was inquiring about, so I was the potential client. It was immediately evident that the person doing the demo had everything enlarged so they could see it better, like HUGE font size. But that's also how it showed to me, so I felt like I was really only seeing a small part of the presentation. If you need reading glasses to see the screen, then get them. Don't change your screen size if you are doing virtual demos.

13. Get rid of the bed:

Please, please get rid of the bed in your background image. Listen, I realize that we all don't have separate office spaces in our homes, and we need to use the space we have, so either use a platform where you can "choose" a virtual background image or change the screen direction so it is not showing the bed. As a side note, clean up the clutter. Be aware of what is showing in the background screen and keep it clean.

14. Angles are important:

Be aware of how properly adjusting the angle of your screen can flatter or flaunt your assets. I also get in a meeting ahead of time so I can move things around, like moving the screen up to make me look thinner. (Yes, it works!) Or you can purchase a computer stand that allows the computer to sit up nice and high—also very flattering. Find the angle that works best for you.

15. Lighting is also crucial:

I am lucky that my office has big windows with natural light but, depending on the time of day, that can also be a detriment. So I quickly look at the lighting as I enter the meeting and close the blinds if the glare is too harsh. I have a lamp right beside me if the opposite is happening and I need a bit of extra light on a dark day or night.

16. Features like chat, record, screen share:

Be aware of features the virtual meeting platform offers, such as chat. I have had clients come into meetings and I can't hear them. It appears they are still muted or they don't have speakers. I can quickly type into the chat feature to tell them to unmute or ask them to give me their cell number. I have recorded sessions as well, which lets the clients take the screen to show me something. So know your way around the platform you are using.

I have spent a lot of time adapting my virtual presentations to make them what they are today. Prospects tell me, "That was a great presentation." I know they are often vetting other agencies, so this is my opportunity to shine and win the sale. **It must be great—not just good.**

It is one thing to connect with a prospect online; it's another thing to close them online. Map it out, perfect it, change things up—make it great. Do what your competitors are not doing. Very few businesses are doing a great job of virtual selling. It could be your chance to stand out.

Last tip: I immediately recap the conversation in an email following the meeting, with examples of what we looked at and some personal notes, so they know it is not a canned response.

 Hot Points to Remember:

- **Sales skills apply online too**
- **Get amazing at virtual presentations**
- **Be great ... not good**

CHAPTER 9 TO-DO LIST

	Get to know all virtual meeting platforms.
	Build a great virtual presentation.
	Look at your background, lighting, angles.
	Record your next presentation and watch it afterwards.

CHAPTER 10

The Sale Is Never Dead

*Our greatest weakness lies in giving
up. The most certain way to succeed
is to try one more time.*

—THOMAS EDISON

I started to play golf about ten years ago. I quickly realized that I was going to have to develop some specific skills to be any good at this game. There is so much strategy in golfing. You need the right clubs, the perfect grip, the proper stance, correct alignment, right swing, and, most important, eye connection! Even after golfing for ten years, I still swing and completely miss the ball at least once a game. I call it a **total miss**.

Why do I miss it? I take my eye off the ball. I am already looking at where it is supposed to go before I even hit it. I must mentally say to myself every time: "Keep your head down. Don't look up. Keep your eye on the ball. Don't try to kill it." Sound familiar? If you're a golfer, you will know exactly what I mean.

Do you ever have a "total miss" in sales?

I see two "total misses" or, if we flip the philosophy, "two opportunities" every day.

They are the follow-up and the last impressions.

Let's start with the follow-up:

The sale is often not made on the first attempt. Yet, very few salespeople have a good follow-up system. First, let's understand why the sale didn't close. There are lots of reasons a sale will not close right away:

- The clients are not ready to buy

- They have additional questions

- They are shopping around for more options

- You did not give them enough value

- They were not the decision makers

- You haven't convinced them you are the best option

- They are too busy, or they don't feel any immediate urgency to buy

I close sales during a demo, or a few days later, a week later, a month later, six months later, or even years later. The sale is never dead. Every salesperson has a different sales cycle, but what I have learned is to never consider the sale as done (even if they have confirmed they bought from someone else, but we'll get to that later in the chapter).

If I have done an actual sales presentation or demo and it did not close right away, I send an immediate recap email thanking them for their time with some examples of our work. I track it all in a master spreadsheet, and I then follow my own follow-up strategy.

20   3 Days, 3 Weeks, 3 Months

Unlike other marketers who will hound potential clients with automated emails that hit them five to seven times in the first fourteen days, I prefer a **gentler approach.**

After three days, I send this message:

> *Hi Dr. Smith, just checking in to see if you had any questions about our marketing program or the examples I sent you.*

After three weeks:

> *Hi Dr. Smith, hope you are doing well. I know it's been a while since we chatted, but I wanted to share some exciting free resources we just added to our website for immediate download. You can find them here: ____. If you are interested in chatting again about your marketing, please reach out.*

After three months:

> *Hi Dr. Smith, Happy Holidays! It's a great time to start planning your marketing strategy for next year. That is why I wanted to share this recorded webinar, as well as a marketing calendar and workbook you can access immediately. We love helping our clients plan a full year of marketing initiatives. If we can assist at all with your marketing for next year, please let us know.*

💬 **My outreach is never aggressive.** My goal is to be a resource and re-engage with them so they want to continue discussions. I use the "give, give, give, ask" process as I build my follow-up scripts, and I track all follow-ups in the database. If they don't respond after the third attempt, I leave them alone, but I add them to our company email list so they will get ongoing communications and marketing from us.

But let me say this: follow-up works for me. I have closed many a sale specifically because I put myself back on the top of the client's mind, thanks to my follow-up. Clients say I seem like I care and that I wanted the business, but that I was willing to share regardless of winning the business. And you know what else? No one else followed up with them. :)

Follow-up to Cold Outreach

I use a similar approach to cold digital outreach. In the last few chapters, you learned about prospecting on email, LinkedIn, Instagram, and Facebook. As many of these have not turned into demos, I follow a different timeline of additional follow-up outreach.

 ## 3 Months, 6 Months, 1 Year

My follow-up efforts are easier now as I keep a very up-to-date master spreadsheet. I can quickly look and see exactly how I connected with the prospect in my last attempt and when. If I am connected with them on multiple channels, I may try a different channel, or the same one. It all depends on how active they seem to be on one or the other.

Because we create so many great giveaways, like recorded webinars, checklists, quizzes, downloadable resources, and more, it makes it super easy to reach back out. I never feel like I am selling. I am truly giving them something that is about helping them in their businesses. This is the reason I rarely, if ever, get pushback. I don't hound people and I don't pressure them. **And I always give them something of value.**

Last Impressions

Follow-up is not just for new prospects you are still trying to win. It can also be for sales you have actually lost (meaning they actually bought from your competitor) and for clients who have left you.

Listen—I hate losing sales. But I hate losing current clients even more. I take it very personally. I have had to learn how to deal with it so I don't react negatively. Here are a couple of stories about why you never "close the door."

Story 1: Losing a BIG Client

Once we get clients, we rarely lose them. We pride ourselves on superior service, attention, quality, and results. We still have most of the clients who started with us in 2015. It is testament to what we do.

That's why I was blindsided when one of our clients gave us notice that they were leaving. There were so many reasons I was surprised. First, I knew them personally, so I thought I would have known if they were unhappy. Second, we were actually doing extra for this client, as they were very influential in the industry, and they were getting amazing results.

I reached out personally to find out why they were leaving and found out they had been wooed away by another agency that told them they could do more than what we were doing, for less money. I knew that was not possible. Our margins are thin, and we were working super hard on this account. There was no way this competitor could live up to these promises. But it was too late to stop them from leaving, so I did what every salesperson in this situation should do:

Wish them well and leave the door open.

Three months later, they called me. They were so disappointed in the new agency. It was a terrible experience. Their results were actually tanking, and the service was not good. The agency was not doing what it said it could do. The client wanted to come back to us and they apologized for doubting that what we did was worth the cost.

What did we do? We warmly welcomed them home.

Lesson: Leave the door open.

Story 2: Losing a BIG Sale

I work hard to get a sale. When I get an actual demo, I am prepared and do a great job of presenting why we are the best choice. I do a ton of research, so I come to the meeting with so much relevant information and intel the prospect is usually very impressed that I have done so much homework on them. I know I show them a lot more than my competitors do.

I had spent a considerable amount of time with this one practice from California. They were two young Optometry practice owners who had started a practice from scratch and were ready to take their online presence to the next level. After the initial demonstration they must have sent me ten different emails with a minimum of five questions on every email. They were doing their own homework, and it was apparent that they were vetting us against some other vendors. Not only did I answer all of their questions, I also arranged two reference calls with a couple of our current clients so they could hear firsthand about the experience of working with us.

After weeks of back and forth they let me know that they were going with another vendor. I asked for some feedback and all they said was that the other vendor had a better price. I did what every salesperson should do in this situation:

 Wish them well and leave the door open.

One year later their contract was up with the other agency, and they reached out. It had not been a great experience and they did not get what they wanted. They were ready to give us a try. They have told me since that they LOVE their new website, LOVE working with our team, and LOVE that we made it so easy to come back to us. One of the doctors told me that even though I had lost the business I was uber professional and I "left them well."

Lesson: Leave them well.

You will lose a few potential clients, and you might even lose a few current clients. How you handle it will dictate if you ever get another chance with them. Salespeople often close the door, sometimes without even realizing they are doing it.

Learn to leave them well. It's hard to not react and get upset. But don't show it. It won't get you anywhere. They may not have a great experience where they have gone or not be happy with the product. So, leave an opening. They might be embarrassed and not sure how to approach you, which is why you should always stay connected and visible.

 Guard your reputation. It's all you have. Be easy to work with. Be kind in every situation. Don't react. It will come back to you tenfold.

🔥 **Hot Points to Remember:**

- **Follow up, follow up, follow up**
- **Leave the door open**
- **Leave them well**

 **CHAPTER 10 TO-DO LIST**

	Track all follow-up in a master spreadsheet or in a sales CRM.
	Develop a system for follow-up: 3 days, 3 weeks, 3 months, or 3 months to 6 months to 1 year.
	Stay connected and visible to clients who have left you.
	Develop a wish-you-well script for when you lose a potential sale.

CHAPTER 11

Be a Digital Road Warrior

Sometimes the most scenic roads in life are the detours you didn't mean to take.

—ANGELA N. BLOUNT

In my first outside sales job with Bausch & Lomb, I would experience life on the road and all it had to offer. I don't think I will ever forget the day they dropped off my company car, a beige Chevrolet Impala. Certainly it wasn't the prettiest or sportiest car, but it was spacious, had a huge trunk, and was great on the roads in the winter. Now, if my friends had just stopped bugging me about being a taxi driver (many taxis are Impalas), things would have been just fine.

It didn't take long for me to realize my car was now my office. I would spend 8+ hours a day driving from appointment to appointment, or on the highway heading to another city in my territory. I actively set up things to make my office more effective. Remember, this is years and years ago, so don't laugh, but I bought a GPS (yes, the one that suctions to the window), a laminated printout of all of my accounts and their contact information, a car caddy organizer to house everything from my coffee to pens and Kleenex—and not to forget a cell phone holder so I could see the calls coming in. Yep, those were some golden years.

Now your car needs to be a **digital office**.

There are many new technologies and advancements that can assist you in turning your car into a working digital office.

Laptop Desk

If you have ever tried to balance your laptop on your lap in the car, you know it is not only uncomfortable, but it is also hard to type. Try doing a Google search for "car desks" and you will be amazed at how many options there are, from desks that can snap onto the steering wheel to console attachments and full pop-up desks that sit on the passenger seat.

Bluetooth Speakerphone

Most vehicles today have the ability to connect via Bluetooth to your phone for hands-free calls. The systems also track your most recent calls and top numbers for easy access. They also allow you to verbally ask to call a person or number and show text messages coming in and allow you to dictate a response.

Power Inverter and USB Ports

Many newer vehicles are coming equipped with extra USB ports that work great for your phone and tablets, but laptops still often need to be plugged in. Look online for options, especially on Amazon, as there are several adapters that have an AC outlet plug-in.

Wi-Fi

With the surge in 5G networks also comes the new wave of connectivity. There's a great article here that talks about all the different ways to get Wi-Fi in your car, from buying a 5G router or a VPN modem to talking with your cell company about different plans that include an unlimited hotspot option. Check it out: https://nectmodem.com/blog/need-internet-in-your-car-learn-about-these-three-ways-to-get-wifi-on-the-road/. Some car manufacturers are also jumping on the car Wi-Fi bandwagon. Tesla, which comes with a Wi-Fi plan, is a great example, and other companies are advertising the "connected car" as the car of the future.

Hotspot Plans

Verizon, Bell, and T-Mobile are just a few of the cell phone providers that are offering annual and monthly hotspot plans to turn your car into a workstation.

Public Wi-Fi

Parking lots outside of cafés or coffee shops sometimes have Wi-Fi and some cities have public Wi-Fi available in certain areas, which means you can park there and enjoy some digital time at no charge. Just be aware that the signals can often vary and have limited strength.

iPad Car Mount

I've found it easy to pull out my iPad to do some quick social prospecting. It's not as big or clunky as my laptop. However, if I am trying to multitask—like eat and prospect—it's hard to hold the iPad, so I purchased a mount. It sits up by the air vent, and I can easily click on the social channels and get to work. Just look for options on Amazon.

Portable Battery Pack

I love portable battery packs as they have saved my butt a few times when I have forgotten to charge my cell phone. I actually keep one in my purse and have charged my phone during an appointment!

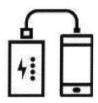

Travel Fan

Air conditioning is great, but sometimes you don't want to keep your car running and running. Buy a battery-operated travel fan.

Headphones

One of the best investments I ever made was a pair of noise-canceling Bose headphones. Great for noisy hotel rooms or flights, they also work great for sitting in busy parking lots and for making phone calls in loud areas. Wireless AirPods work well too.

Mobile Printer

Remember when printers were the size of a closet? Well, now they are the size of a book. If you need to access printers for reports, order forms, or other work-related documents, then invest in a mobile printer. It will likely save you time and money over stopping at an office supply store.

Coffee and Food

What's an office without coffee? If you spend a significant amount of time in your car, you might want to invest in some new travel options, such as a cooler you can plug into the AC adapter or battery-operated coffee makers. There are even blenders that are travel friendly, for whipping up a protein shake or two. Find them all online with a quick Google or Amazon search.

Now you have your car set up as a digital office. Let's talk about how to utilize time. As you head back out to the road, don't forget all these amazing tips we have been teaching you about digital prospecting. These are the times to ensure traditional meets digital. Take advantage of the pockets of available time you have on the road every day to continue to do your digital due diligence.

1. **Drive Time**

Every day, we spend a ton of time driving. Do some cold calling on the road. Have phone numbers of prospects pre-programmed on your phone and get calling. It's also a great way to follow up with prospects who have not closed.

2. Early Arrival

How many of you arrive at an appointment and you have ten to fifteen minutes of time, or you are sitting in a waiting room waiting for your appointment? Use this time to connect with ten new clients on LinkedIn or to like ten new Facebook target business pages. There's a lot you can do in ten minutes.

3. Hotel Time

If you spend nights as part of your travel, utilize the time. I would grab some takeout and head back to my room. Then I would catch up on all my emails and text messages and I would also do some digital prospecting as I sit and watch TV. I could easily hit up ten direct messages on Instagram and scan all the Facebook groups I follow to see if there are any messages around marketing and social media.

4. Fly Time

I spend a lot of time flying, especially during conference season. I get a lot done in airports and on planes, as it seems like available time that is there for the taking. I often head to the airport early, get checked in, go through security, and hit the airport lounge or a coffee shop to get working. I can bang off a ton of emails and social prospecting in an hour or two. Then when I get on the plane, I pay for the Wi-Fi and get to work. It's amazing how a four-hour flight flies by when you're absorbed in work.

5. Coffee and Mealtime

Every Starbucks has Wi-Fi and really, so do most restaurants and pubs these days. I used to hate eating alone on the road until I started to turn it into a working meal. I always take my laptop into the restaurant and work while waiting for the meal.

The lesson you learned throughout the book was that you can connect with ten times more prospects through digital methods in a day than through traditional ones. I remember running from appointment to appointment, only to see five accounts or clients in a day. Digitally, I can hit another one hundred in a day. Traditional methods are still required and, in many cases, mandated by your company, but pair it up now with digital and you will see 10x the sales and new clients.

You are now a digital sales road warrior. Get connecting and selling.

 Hot Points to Remember:

- **Traditional needs to meet digital**
- **Build a digital office in your car**
- **Use your time wisely**

✓ CHAPTER 11 TO-DO LIST

	Look for a car laptop desk.
	Invest in Wi-Fi for your car.
	Check with your cell phone company on hotspot plans.
	Get a portable battery pack.

Conclusion

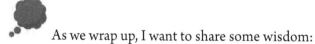I knew that I had to share the secret to digital sales success after I experienced such momentum with the 10 + 10 Sales System. I wanted to share skills that other salespeople can learn and use to grow their connections to get to that targeted decision maker in the new normal we live in. And how it is the new way of sales!

The new way of sales is digital and changing every day. You need to constantly find new ways to sell if you want to stay competitive.

Besides wanting to share the secrets of digital sales success, I also want to help salespeople. I know that every time I actively help other people succeed, it helps me succeed.

I hope we stay connected now that you have finished the book. In fact, I hope this is not goodbye. I hope we are lifelong sales buddies. We are going to be friends for a long time! That means you are following me on LinkedIn or Instagram and joining my Facebook group to dive deeper into sales tips with other people who are doing exactly what you are doing, every day. I also encourage you to take me up on the free resources available on my website: www.thedigitalsalesrep.com.

As we wrap up, I want to share some wisdom:

It is my belief that we get out of this life what we put into it. We don't get what we don't ask for, and actions speak louder than words. Just get on the digital channels we talked about and make some things happen. There are a lot of people who will read this book, but you can be the one who takes the advice and puts it into action.

Over the years I have been called a lot of things: relentless, tenacious, demanding, driven, innovative, inspiring, a perfectionist, pushy, giving, ambitious, and a workaholic, just to name a few. Thank you ... I happily reply to any of them. If you are going to be successful, you will need to be called some of these things. :)

I have had a lot of obstacles. I moved out at eighteen with nothing and made it on my own. I lost both my parents in my thirties to cancer. I was diagnosed with stage 4 ovarian cancer eight months after starting our company and I beat it. I've had people try to bring down our company but have prevailed by taking the high road and not reacting.

Don't let obstacles stop you in your tracks. Find a door, climb the mountain, borrow the money, build a bridge, or, in other words, do whatever it takes to get through and get going.

I have seen a lot of opportunities. In fact, there has never been a shortage of opportunity. I am thankful every day that I stepped out of my comfort zone and into the unknown. I took my first sales job at B&L where my income skyrocketed. I started my own training and consulting company where I landed a vice president's role that would be one of the highlights of my career. But the biggest opportunity and the scariest was to leave all that and start a marketing agency from scratch. Don't just see opportunity, seize it, learn more, move forward, get involved, take the leap, and get out of your comfort zone. **Have no regrets.**

I have had many mentors. Mentors have been such a gift. Be open to learning, to heed direction, to hear advice and sometimes criticism, and to be coachable. I hope this book will be a mentor to you in your sales journey.

If you learned one golden nugget from this book that helps you make a sale or moves you forward in some way, then I feel I have done my job. Go forth and get selling.

Last tips not to forget:

1. **Learn how to get and keep the attention from your target audience:**

Use the tips we gave you in the book to stand out and grab attention. Be someone in your industry who people know and recognize.

2. **Stop pitching—start helping and become a resource:**

There is nothing that has helped me more in sales than to reroute to being a resource first and foremost. It actually makes sales easier.

3. **Go for the gold:**

The more you try anything, the more likely you are to hit gold.

Sales is all about effort, day in and day out. The more effort you put in, the more results will come out of it. Don't be mediocre; be a gold star.

4. **Use no-pressure sales tactics—they work:**

Be different from the high-pressure salespeople in your circle. Give, give, give, then ask. Give value, build the relationship, make being connected to you easy with no pressure.

5. **Build the list and hit the list:**

If you have a list of target clients, go after it. If you don't, build your own list and hit the list every day.

6. LinkedIn is your secret advantage:

Every salesperson needs to know, understand, and utilize LinkedIn. If someone said all of your prospective clients were at a party, you would go to the party and mingle. Well, that's LinkedIn.

7. Follow-up is key:

Build a system to follow up with all prospective clients, first, to stay top of mind, but second because you never know when someone is ready to pull the trigger.

8. Leave things well:

You won't make every sale at the moment you're trying to close it, but that does not mean there may not be opportunities in the future. Leave the door open and leave things well. Make it easy for a client to come back to you.

 Cheers!

Acknowledgments

It's fitting that the acknowledgments are the last thing you write after you finish writing your book because at this point you are mentally exhausted but excited. You also realize through the writing how many people have touched parts of your book, from the stories and the lessons to the quotes.

And it is only fitting that we have a place to thank them.

To the most important person in my life, my husband, Al. I can't thank you enough for your love and endless support. You have always let me do anything I set my mind to. You never question my motives, even when they seem a bit crazy, like leaving a very lucrative vice president role to start a company from scratch. I love that you have such belief in me and help me get through the stresses with your calm and optimistic nature.

To my family, starting with my mom and dad, who are looking down from Heaven. I am so grateful for your loving upbringing and instilled values that still drive my actions daily. My sister Lynda: you are my best friend, my rock, my confidante, and the most giving person alive. You are always doing something for someone else and you have done so much for me in our lifetime together. My brother Pat: your never-give-up attitude and your desire to make sure life is fun are what make you my favorite brother. My younger brother Ken (really, you are my favorite brother, but don't tell Pat): you remind me so much of Dad. You are always smiling, always happy and calm. You have his hard-work ethic and this gentle nature; you are one of the nicest people I know. To my other brother Larry, RIP. To Pat and Diane: thanks for being great in-laws, for the love and support you show to your family. You are selfless in wanting to give and give to your kids all the time.

To my BFFs—Cheri, Lynda, Vanessa, Gloria, Sylvia, Donna, Tamara, and Brenda ... thanks for the daily chatline, for the years of amazing fun memories, and for your unwavering friendship and support. You are my stress relievers.

 To a few of my mentors over the years:

Marina Vitelli ... RIP. You knew how to bring out the best in people and push them.

Barbara Mills ... RIP. I never got the chance to tell you how much you affected me and made me step over fear.

Patricia Bassendowske ... you are a part of my success. You always helped others be successful and I am nothing without your friendship and mentorship.

Shawn Larsen ... you were such a great leader to work for. You held people accountable, but you let them do their thing. It was working for you that allowed me to see what I could truly do because you believed in me.

Kim Pearce ... thank you for being my cheerleader. You were always so encouraging and positive.

Ken Barbet ... I learnt so much from you. You gave me such freedom to do what I do well. You are one of the smartest businesspeople I have ever worked with. You get it!

To my current business partners:

Karim ... we have taken this little start-up to some amazing levels and I am so appreciative of you and your skills. If I had to do your job, we would be a financial mess, so thank you for doing what you do for our business. I also appreciate that we have found a friendship and respect that can only be born out of some challenges and difficult times. We survived and thrived. Thanks, Buddy.

Kevin … I can honestly say you are such a great leader and innovator as well as a kick-ass partner. It's hard to believe we are 6+ years in and business is rocking. I love how we have all found our own niche in how to grow this company, and with you at the helm it has grown leaps and bounds. You are a friend, an ally, and an inspiration to me. I am grateful every day that we met and started this business.

To my many other friends, extended family, colleagues, work family, and anyone else who has been a part of my life … thank you. You have probably affected some part of this book in some way.

About the Author

Trudi Charest is the Co-Founder of Marketing4ECPs, a digital marketing agency focused on building digital advertising for the eye care industry. Trudi is well known for designing, developing, and facilitating training and marketing programs for eye care professionals across North America.

Trudi is a Licensed Optician with over 25 years of eye care experience. She also holds a Human Resource Management certificate from the University of Calgary. Her experience before starting Marketing4ECPs in 2015 included corporate training in retail optical, territory management for Bausch & Lomb, Clinical Consulting with Optos, and the role of VP of Marketing and Training for Eye Recommend, one of Canada's leading Optometric buying groups.

Trudi was one of Vision Monday's "2019 Most Influential Women" in the optical industry. She is an active OWA (Optical Women's Association) member and was elected to the board of directors in 2021. She is an international speaker, author, industry consultant, and business innovator.

Connect with Trudi:

- LinkedIn: https://www.linkedin.com/in/trudicharest/
- Instagram:https://www.instagram.com/digitalsalesrep/https://www.instagram.com/eyecaremarketer/
- Website: https://www.thedigitalsalesrep.com
- Email: hello@thedigitalsalesrep.com

Manufactured by Amazon.ca
Bolton, ON